Śrī Brahma-saṁhitā

Publications of the Bhaktivedānta Book Trust

BOOKS by His Divine Grace
A. C. Bhaktivedanta Swami Prabhupāda

Bhagavad-gītā As It Is
Śrīmad-Bhāgavatam (completed by disciples)
Śrī Caitanya-caritāmṛta
Kṛṣṇa, the Supreme Personality of Godhead
Teachings of Lord Caitanya
The Nectar of Devotion
The Nectar of Instruction
Śrī Īśopaniṣad
Light of the Bhāgavata
Easy Journey to Other Planets
Teachings of Lord Kapila, the Son of Devahūti
Teachings of Queen Kuntī
Message of Godhead
The Science of Self-Realization
The Perfection of Yoga
Beyond Birth and Death
On the Way to Kṛṣṇa
Rāja-vidyā: The King of Knowledge
Elevation to Kṛṣṇa Consciousness
Kṛṣṇa Consciousness: The Matchless Gift
Kṛṣṇa Consciousness: The Topmost Yoga System
Perfect Questions, Perfect Answers
Life Comes from Life
The Nārada-bhakti-sūtra (completed by disciples)
The Mukunda-mālā-stotra (completed by disciples)
Geetār-gān (Bengali)
Vairāgya-vidyā (Bengali)
Buddhi-yoga (Bengali)
Bhakti-ratna-boli (Bengali)
Back to Godhead magazine (founder)

BOOKS compiled from the teachings of His Divine Grace
A. C. Bhaktivedanta Swami Prabhupāda after his lifetime

Search for Liberation
Bhakti-yoga, the Art of Eternal Love
The Journey of Self-Discovery
Dharma, the Way of Transcendence
The Hare Kṛṣṇa Challenge
Renunciation Through Wisdom
A Second Chance
Beyond Illusion and Doubt
Civilization and Transcendence
Spiritual Yoga
The Laws of Nature
The Quest for Enlightenment

Śrī Brahma-saṁhitā

His Divine Grace
Bhaktisiddhānta Sarasvatī
Gosvāmī Ṭhākura

THE BHAKTIVEDANTA BOOK TRUST
LOS ANGELES • STOCKHOLM • MUMBAI • SYDNEY

Readers interested in the subject matter of this book are invited by the International Society for Krishna Consciousness to correspond with its Secretary at one of the following addresses:

International Society for Krishna Consciousness
P.O. Box 341445
Los Angeles, California 90034, USA
Telephone: 1-800-927-4152 (inside USA);
1-310-837-5283 (outside USA)
e-mail: bbt.usa@krishna.com • web: www.krishna.com

First printing, 1985: 10,000
Second printing, 1991: 5,000
Current printing, 2013: 5,000

Printed in China

ISBN: 978-0-89213-145-4

Contents

Introduction

The origins of the text known as the *Brahma-saṁhitā* are lost in cosmic antiquity. According to Vedic tradition, these "Hymns of Brahmā" were recited or sung countless millennia ago by the first created being in the universe, just prior to the act of creation. The text surfaced and entered calculable history early in the sixteenth century, when it was discovered by a pilgrim exploring the manuscript library of an ancient temple in what is now Kerala state in South India. Prior to the introduction of the printing press, texts like the *Brahma-saṁhitā* existed only in manuscript form, painstakingly handwritten by scribes and kept under brahminical custodianship in temples, where often they were worshiped as *śāstra*—Deity, or God incarnate in holy scripture.

The pilgrim who rescued the *Brahma-saṁhitā* from obscurity was no ordinary pilgrim, and His pilgrimage was not meant, as is the custom, for self-purification but for world-purification. He was Śrī Caitanya Mahāprabhu—saint, mystic, religious reformer, and full incarnation of the Supreme Lord, Śrī Kṛṣṇa, descending into the present epoch for the salvation of all souls. At the time of His discovery of the text, Śrī Caitanya was touring South India, preaching His message of love of Kṛṣṇa and promulgating the practice of *saṅkīrtana*, congregational singing of the holy names of God. Śrī Caitanya commenced this tour shortly after becoming a monk (*sannyāsī*), at age twenty-four, and the tour lasted approximately two years. After a southward journey from Purī (in Orissa State) that carried Him to holy places such as Śrī Raṅga-kṣetra, Setubandha Rāmeśvara, and finally Kanyākumārī (Cape Comorin), he turned northward and, traveling along the bank of the Payasvinī River in Travancore state, reached the temple of Ādi-keśava in Trivandrum district.

Śrī Caitanya's principal biographer, Kṛṣṇadāsa Kavirāja Gosvāmī, writes in *Caitanya-caritāmṛta* (*Madhya-līlā*, Ch. 9) that upon beholding the holy image of Ādi-keśava (Kṛṣṇa) in the temple, Caitanya was overwhelmed with spiritual ecstasy, offered fervent prayers, and chanted and danced in rapture, a wondrous sight that was received with astonished appreciation by the devotees there. After discussing esoteric spiritual matters among some highly advanced devotees present, Śrī Caitanya found "one chapter of the *Brahma-saṁhitā*" (what we now have as the *Brahma-saṁhitā* is, according to tradition, only one of a hundred chapters composing an epic work lost to humanity). Upon discovering the manuscript, Śrī Caitanya felt great ecstasy and fell into an intense mystic rapture that overflowed onto the physical realm, producing a profusion of tears, trembling, and perspiration. (We would search the literature of the world in vain to find a case in which the discovery of a lost book inspired such unearthly exhilaration!) Intuiting the *Brahma-saṁhitā* to be a "most valuable jewel," He employed a scribe in hand-copying the manuscript and departed with the copy for His return journey to the north.

Upon His return to Purī (*Madhya-līlā*, Ch. 11), Śrī Caitanya presented the *Brahma-saṁhitā* to appreciative followers like Rāmānanda Rāya and Vāsudeva Datta, for whom Caitanya arranged copies to be made. As word of the discovery of the text spread within the Vaiṣṇava community, "each and every Vaiṣṇava" copied it. Gradually, the *Brahma-saṁhitā* was "broadcast everywhere" and became one of the major texts of the Gauḍīya-Vaiṣṇava canon. "There is no scripture equal to the *Brahma-saṁhitā* as far as the final spiritual conclusion is concerned," exults Kṛṣṇadāsa Kavirāja. "Indeed, that scripture is the supreme revelation of the glories of Lord Govinda, for it reveals the topmost knowledge about Him. Since all conclusions are briefly presented in *Brahma-saṁhitā*, it is essential among all the Vaiṣṇava literatures." (*Madhya-līlā* 9.239–40)

Now, what of the text itself? What are its contents? A synopsis of the *Brahma-saṁhitā* is provided by Śrīla Prabhupāda, founder-*ācārya* of the Kṛṣṇa consciousness movement, in his commentary to the *Caitanya-caritāmṛta*. It is quoted here in full:

> In [the *Brahma-saṁhitā*], the philosophical conclusion of *acintya-bhedābheda-tattva* (simultaneous oneness and difference) is presented. [It] also presents methods of devotional service, the eighteen-syllable Vedic hymn, discourses on the soul, the Supersoul and fruitive activity, an explanation of Kāma-gāyatrī, *kāma-bīja* and the original Mahā-Viṣṇu, and a detailed description of the spiritual world, specifically Goloka Vṛndāvana. The *Brahma-saṁhitā* also explains the demigod Gaṇeśa, Garbhodakaśāyī Viṣṇu, the origin of the Gāyatrī *mantra*, the form of Govinda and His transcendental position and abode, the living entities, the highest goal, the goddess Durgā, the meaning of austerity, the five gross elements, love of Godhead, impersonal Brahman, the initiation of Lord Brahmā, and the vision of transcendental love enabling one to see the Lord. The steps of devotional service are also explained. The mind, *yoga-nidrā*, the goddess of fortune, devotional service in spontaneous ecstasy, incarnations beginning with Lord Rāmacandra, Deities, the conditioned soul and its duties, the truth about Lord Viṣṇu, prayers, Vedic hymns, Lord Śiva, the Vedic literature, personalism and impersonalism, good behavior, and many other subjects are also discussed. There is also a description of the sun and the universal form of the Lord. All these subjects are conclusively explained in a nutshell in the *Brahma-saṁhitā*. (*Madhya-līlā* 9.239–240)

In spite of the seeming topical complexity of the text, the essential core of the *Brahma-saṁhitā* consists of a brief description of the enlightenment of Lord Brahmā by Lord Śrī Kṛṣṇa, followed by Brahmā's extraordinarily beautiful prayers elucidating the content of his revelation: an earthly, beatific vision of the Supreme Personality of Godhead, Lord Śrī Kṛṣṇa, and His eternal, transcendental abode, Goloka Vṛndāvana, beyond the material cosmos. This core of the text stretches through verses twenty-nine to fifty-six, and a brief, subsequent exposition by Lord Kṛṣṇa on the path of *kṛṣṇa-bhakti*, love of God, brings the text to a close.

The *Brahma-saṁhitā's* account of Brahmā's enlightenment is quite interesting and can be summarized here. When Lord Viṣṇu (Garbhodakaśāyī Viṣṇu) desires to recreate the universe,[1] a divine golden lotus flower grows from His navel, and Brahmā is born from this lotus. As he is not born from parents, Brahmā is known as "Svayambhū" ("self-existent" or "unoriginated"). Upon his emergence from the lotus, Brahmā begins—in preparation for his role as secondary creator—to contemplate the act of cosmic creation[2] but, seeing only darkness about, is bewildered in the performance of his duty. Sarasvatī, the goddess of learning, appears before him and instructs him to meditate upon the *kāma-bīja mantra* (*klīṁ kṛṣṇāya govindāya gopījana-vallabhāya svāhā*), promising that this *mantra* "will assuredly fulfill your heart's desire." Lord Brahmā thus meditates upon Lord Kṛṣṇa in His spiritual realm and hears the divine sound of Kṛṣṇa's flute. The Kāma-gāyatrī *mantra* (*klīṁ kāmadevāya vidmahe puṣpa-bāṇāya dhīmahi tan no 'naṅgaḥ pracodayāt*), the "mother of the *Vedas*," is made manifest from the sound of Kṛṣṇa's flute, and Brahmā, thus initiated by the supreme primal preceptor Him-

1 According to the *Purāṇas*, the material cosmos is created and destroyed in a perpetual cycle through eternity, and so the act of creation is not a one-time affair but one that is repeated an infinite number of times.

2 Once the physical universe and its constituent parts are brought into being by Lord Viṣṇu, Brahmā's role in the creation act is to evolve the multifarious types of bodily forms (species) to be inhabited by the innumerable conditioned living beings (*jīvas*) in accordance with their previous *karma*—actions performed by them during their existence in previous millennia.

self, begins to chant the Gāyatrī. (As Śrīla Prabhupāda puts it, "When the sound vibration of Kṛṣṇa's flute is expressed through the mouth of Brahmā, it becomes *gāyatrī*" [*Teachings of Lord Caitanya*, p. 325]). Enlightened by meditation upon the sacred Gāyatrī, Brahmā "became acquainted with the expanse of the ocean of truth." Inspired by his profound and sublime realizations, his heart overflowing with devotion and transcendental insight, Lord Brahmā spontaneously begins to offer a series of poem-prayers to the source of his enlightenment and object of his devotion, Lord Śrī Kṛṣṇa. These exquisite verses form the heart of the *Brahma-saṁhitā*.

There is nothing vague about Brahmā's description of the Lord and His abode. No dim, nihilistic nothingness, no blinding bright lights, no wispy, dreamy visions of harps and clouds; rather, a vibrant, luminescent world in transcendental color, form, and sound—a sublimely variegated spiritual landscape populated by innumerable blissful, eternally liberated souls reveling in spiritual cognition, sensation, and emotion, all in relationship with the all-blissful, all-attractive Personality of Godhead. Here are samples:

I worship Govinda [Kṛṣṇa], the primeval Lord, the first progenitor who is tending the cows, yielding all desire, in abodes built with spiritual gems, surrounded by millions of purpose trees, always served with great reverence and affection by hundreds of thousands of *lakṣmīs* or *gopīs*. (*Brahma-saṁhitā* 5.29)

I worship Govinda, the primeval Lord, who is adept in playing on His flute, with blooming eyes like lotus petals with head decked with peacock's feather, with the figure of beauty tinged with the hue of blue clouds, and His unique loveliness charming millions of Cupids. (*Brahma-saṁhitā* 5.30)

I worship [Goloka Vṛndāvana] . . . where every tree is a transcendental purpose tree; where the soil is the purpose gem, all water is nectar, every word is a song, every gait is a dance, the flute is the favorite attendant, . . . where numberless milk cows always emit transcendental oceans of milk . . . (*Brahma-saṁhitā* 5.56)

The commentator reminds us (Text 56) that in the transcendental region of Goloka are found the same elements as are found in the mundane worlds, but in their highest purity and beauty: "... trees and creepers, mountains, rivers and forests, water, speech, movement, music of the flute, the sun and the moon, tasted and taste ... " Kṛṣṇa's divine abode, Goloka Vṛndāvana, is the *world* in the fullest and realest sense.

There are those who will have difficulty with Brahmā's highly graphic and personalistic depiction of the spiritual world and of the liberated state. Some, for instance, whose conception of transcendence is determined by a certain logical fallacy based on the arbitrary assumption that spirit is the literal opposite of matter (and thus that because matter has form and variety, spirit must necessarily be formless and unvariegated), conceive of ultimate reality as some sort of divine emptiness. However, any conception of transcendence that projects or analogizes from our limited sensory and cognitive experience within the material world is, by its very nature, limited and speculative and thus unreliable. No accumulated quantity of sense data within this world can bring us to knowledge of what lies beyond it. Residents of the material world cannot get even a clue of transcendence, argues our *Brahma-saṁhitā* commentator, "by moving earth and heaven through their organic senses" (p. xvii).

The *Brahma-saṁhitā* teaches that transcendence, truth, ultimate reality can be apprehended only by the mercy of the supreme transcendental entity, the Absolute Truth Himself, and that perception of the ultimate reality is a function not of speculative reason but of direct spiritual cognition through divine revelation. This revelation is evolved through *bhakti*, pure, selfless love of God. Only by such spiritual devotion can Kṛṣṇa be seen: "I worship Govinda, the primeval Lord ... whom the pure devotees see in their heart of hearts with the eye of devotion tinged with the salve of love" (verse 38). Further, as our commentator explains, "the form of Kṛṣṇa is visible [to the eye of the pure spiritual self] in proportion to its purification by the practice of devotion" (p. 71). *Bhakti* as a state of consciousness, then, is attained through *bhakti* as a practice, a discipline. For this reason, Lord Kṛṣṇa, in His response to Brahmā at the end of the text, summarizes the path of *bhakti* in five aphorisms. This devotional discipline goes far beyond conventional piety. It necessitates "constant endeavor for self-realization" (verse 59) involving both a turning from worldly, sense-gratificatory activities as well as sincere absorption in spiritual practices and behavior, under the guidance of authorized scripture. Through such practice, then, the materialist is purified of his tendency toward philosophical negation and comes to understand the nature of positive transcendence.

Others will find Lord Brahmā's vision of the spiritual realm problematic for a related, but perhaps more subjective, emotional reason that goes to the heart of the human condition. There is a kind of ontological anxiety, a conscious or subconscious apprehension about beingness or existence itself, that goes along with the embodied life-in-the-world—that accompanies the soul's descent into the temporal, endlessly changing world of matter. Material bodies and minds are subjected to a huge variety of objective and subjective discomfitures, unpleasantries, and abject sufferings within the material world. Viewed philosophically, embodied personhood, false-self (*ahaṅkāra*), is, to a greater or lesser degree, innately a condition of suffering. Because personal existence has been experienced by materialists as essentially painful, writes Prabhupāda in his *Bhagavad-gītā* commentary, "the conception of retaining the personality after liberation from matter frightens them. When they are informed that spiritual life is also individual and personal, they become afraid of becoming persons again, and so they naturally prefer a kind of merging into the impersonal void" (4.10, purport). Entering the path of *bhakti*, however, such persons can gradually begin to experience their real, spiritual selves and a release from egoistic anxiety. In that purified state, they become able to relish Brahmā's vision of blissful, personal spiritual existence in Goloka.

Still others, however, might criticize the *Brahma-saṁhitā* on the grounds that the text, being quite specific and concrete in its depiction, merely offers another limited, sectarian view of God and His abode—a view in conflict with other, similarly limited views. Such persons prefer a kind of generic Deity who doesn't offend variant theological views with definable, personal attributes. *Brahma-saṁhitā*, however, is not a polemic against "competing" conceptions of the Deity (except those, of course, which would deny His transcendental personhood). Vaiṣṇava tradition does not dismiss images of the Divine derived from authoritative scripture from beyond its own cultural and conceptual borders. It respects any sincere effort at serving the Supreme Person, although naturally it holds its own texts as most comprehensive and authoritative. It promotes neither an arrogant sectarianism that would constrain transcendence to exclusive cultural, ideational, or linguistic forms (and burn a few heretics) nor a syncretistic ecumenism that would try to pacify all claimants on the truth by departicularizing it into bland vagueness. Let the syncretists and the sectarians come together to appreciate, at least, the aesthetic magnificence of Brahmā's theistic epiphany.

What we are experiencing through Lord Brahmā in his *saṁhitā* is not mystic hallucination or quaint mythologizing or an exercise in pious wishful thinking. We are getting a glimpse, however dimmed by our own insensitivities, into the spiritual world as seen by one whose eyes are "tinged with the salve of love." We are seeing, through Brahmā, an eternal, transcendental world of which the present world is a mere reflection. Goloka is infinitely more real than the shadowy world we perceive daily through our narrow senses. Brahmā's vision of the spiritual realm is not his alone. It is shared by all those who give themselves fully unto the loving service of Lord Kṛṣṇa—though Brahmā admits that Goloka is known "only to a very few self-realized souls in this world" (verse 56). We are not asked to accept Brahmā's account of transcendence uncritically and dogmatically but to avail ourselves of the spiritual discipline, *bhakti-yoga*, that will gradually lead us to our own experiential understanding of this highest truth. The publishers of this small volume hope that a careful perusal of the text will inspire *bhakti* in the heart of the reader. It should be noted that the *Brahma-saṁhitā* is an advanced spiritual text and is more easily understood once one has some familiarity with texts such as the *Bhagavad-gītā*, *Śrīmad-Bhāgavatam*, *Caitanya-caritāmṛta*, and *Bhakti-rasāmṛta-sindhu*.

This volume is a new and expanded edition of an English-language *Brahma-saṁhitā* edition published in India in 1932 by the Gaudiya Math (a Caitanya-Vaiṣṇava religious institution), with subsequent reprints in 1958 and 1973. These editions featured the English translation and commentary of Śrīla Bhaktisiddhānta Sarasvatī Gosvāmī (1874–1937), a great Vaiṣṇava saint and scholar of wide repute and the founder of the Gaudiya Math. It was Bhaktisiddhānta Sarasvatī who inspired the founder and spiritual master of the Hare Kṛṣṇa movement, his dearmost disciple Śrīla A.C. Bhaktivedanta Swami Prabhupāda, to journey to and teach Kṛṣṇa consciousness in the West, beginning in 1965.

As per Śrīla Prabhupāda's instructions regarding the publication of this volume, Bhaktisiddhānta Sarasvatī's somewhat technical and sometimes difficult prose has been left intact and virtually untouched. Fearing that any editorial (grammatical and stylistic) tampering with Bhaktisiddhānta's text might result in inadvertent changes in meaning. Prabhupāda asked that it be left as it is, and the editors of this volume have complied with his wishes. Only typographical errors have been corrected, capitalization has been standardized, Sanskrit terms in *devanāgarī* script appearing within the English text has been transliterated, and already transliterated terms have been adjusted to international standards.

In this edition, the original *devanāgarī* text is shown for each verse of the *Brahma-saṁhitā*, followed by roman transliteration, then by a word-for-word translation into English. (The original Indian edition lacked the later two features.) These, in turn, are followed by Bhaktisiddhānta Sarasvatī's full English translation and commentary. His commentary closely follows that of his great father, Śrīla Bhaktivinoda Ṭhākura (1838–1914), the great Vaiṣṇava saint, reformer, and prolific scholar who initiated a revival of pure Caitanya-Vaiṣṇavism during the latter part of the nineteenth century.

Finally, an index and glossary have been added for the convenience of the reader, as well as several color plates.

The Indian edition of the *Brahma-saṁhitā* included the complete text, in Sanskrit, of the commentary of Jīva Gosvāmī, the great Caitanyite philosopher, but that has been excluded from this edition because, in light of the relative few in the West who would benefit from this inclusion, it was decided that the necessary doubling of the volume's size and price would be disadvantageous.

In his commentary to the twenty-eighth verse of the text, Bhaktisiddhānta Sarasvatī writes that Lord Caitanya "taught this hymn to His favorite disciples inasmuch as it fully contains all the transcendental truths regarding Vaiṣṇava philosophy," and he asks his readers to "study and try to enter into the spirit of this hymn with great care and attention, as a regular daily function." His disciple Śrīla Prabhupāda was very fond of Brahmā's prayers to Lord Kṛṣṇa (. . . *govindam ādi-puruṣaṁ tam ahaṁ bhajāmi*), and there are several recordings of Prabhupāda singing these prayers with obvious, intense devotion. The publishers join with the commentator in inviting readers to dive deeply into the sweet, transcendental ocean of Brahmā's hymns as a daily meditation.

—Śubhānanda dāsa

Foreword

The materialistic demeanor cannot possibly stretch to the transcendental autocrat who is ever inviting the fallen conditioned souls to associate with Him through devotion or eternal serving mood. The phenomenal attractions are often found to tempt sentient beings to enjoy the variegated position which is opposed to undifferenced monism. People are so much apt to indulge in transitory speculations even when they are to educate themselves on a situation beyond their empiric area or experiencing jurisdiction. The esoteric aspect often knocks them to trace out immanence in their outward inspection of transitory and transformable things. This impulse moves them to fix the position of the immanent to an indeterminate impersonal entity, no clue of which could be discerned by moving earth and heaven through their organic senses.

The lines of this booklet will surely help such puzzled souls in their march towards the personality of the immanent lying beyond their sensuous gaze of inspection. The very first stanza of this publication will revolutionize their reserved ideas when the nomenclature of the Absolute is put before them as "Kṛṣṇa." The speculative mind would show a tendency of offering some other attributive name to designate the unknown object. They will prefer to brand Him by their experience as the "creator of this universe,""the entity beyond phenomena"—far off the reference of any object of nature and void of all transformation. So they will urge that the very fountainhead should have no conceivable designation except to show a direction of the invisible, and inaudible untouchable, nonfragrant and unperceivable object. But they will not desist from contemplating on the object with their poor fund of experience. The interested enquirer will be found to hanker after the records left by erudite savants to incompatible hallucinative views of savage demonstration. In comparing the different names offered by different thoughts of mankind, a particular judge would decide in favor of some nomenclature which will suit best his limited and specific whims. The slave mentality of an individual will no doubt offer invective assertions to the rest who will be appealing to him for a revelation of his decision. To remedy this evil, the hymns of the accepted progenitor of the phenomena would do great help in taking up the question of nomenclature which is possessed of adequate power to dispel all imaginations drawn out of their experiencing the phenomena by their tentative exploitations.

The first hymn will establish the supremacy of the Absolute Truth, if His substratum is not shot by the bullets of limited time, ignorance and uncomfortable feeling, as well as by recognizing the same as an effect instead of accepting Him as the prime cause. He will be satisfied to mark that the object of their determination is the par-excellent Supreme Lord Śrī Kṛṣṇa who has eternally embodied Himself in His ever-presence, all-blissful, all-pervasive perfected knowledge as the very fountainhead of all prime causes of unending nonbeginning time, the supplying fosterer of all entities, viz., mundane and transcendental.

The subsequent lines will go to determine the different aspects of the Absolute, who are but emanations of the supreme fountainhead Kṛṣṇa, the attractive entity of all entities. Moreover, the derivative proclamation of the nomenclature will indicate the plane of uninterrupted, unending, transcendental felicity and the nomenclature Himself is the source of the two components which go by the names of efficient and material causes. The very transcendental name "Kṛṣṇa" is known as the embodiment of all the transcendental eternal *rasas* as well as the origin of all eclipsed conceptions of interrupted *rasas* found in the mentality of animated beings which are successfully depicted by litterateurs and rhetoricians for our mundane speculation.

The verses of *Brahma-saṁhitā* are a full elucidation of the origination of phenomenal and noumenic conceptions. The hymns of the incarnated prime potency has dealt fully with the monotheistic speculations of different schools which are busy to give an outer cover of an esoteric concoction without any reference to the true eternal aspect of transcendental nontransformable and imperishable manifestation of the immanent. The hymns have also dealt with different partial aspects of the personality of the Absolute who is quite isolated from the conception of the enjoyers of this phenomenal world.

A very close attention and a comparative study of all prevailing thoughts and conceptions will relieve and enlighten all—be he a materialist, a downright atheist, an agnostic, a sceptic, a naturalist, a pantheist or a panentheist—busy with their knowledge of three dimensions only by their speculative exertions.

This booklet is only the fifth chapter of the Hymns of Brahmā which were recorded in a hundred chapters. The Supreme Lord Śrī Caitanya picked up this chapter from the temple of Ādi-keśava at Tiruvattar, a village lying under the government of Travancore, for the assurance of all God-loving, and especially Kṛṣṇa-loving, people in this conditioned jurisdiction. This booklet can easily be compared with another book which passes by the name of *Śrīmad-Bhāgavatam*. Though it has got a reference in the pantheon of *Purāṇas*, the *Bhāgavatam* corroborates the same idea of this *Pañcarātra*.

The devotees should consider that these two books tend to the identical Kṛṣṇa who is the fountainhead of all transcendental and mundane entities and has a manifestive exhibition of the plenary variegatedness.

Aspersions of calumniation are restricted in the limited world, whereas transcendence cannot admit such angularities being an angle of 180 degrees or void of any angular discrepancies.

The publisher is carried away to the realm of gratitude when his stores of publication are scrutinized. Ṭhākura Bhaktivinoda has given an elucidatory purport of the conception of the most sublime fountainhead of all entities in Bengali, and one of his devout followers has rendered that into English for propagatory purpose. The purports and the translations are traced to the backgrounds of the writings of Śrīla Jīva Gosvāmī, a contemporary follower of the Supreme Lord Śrī Kṛṣṇa Caitanya. The emotional aspirations will find fair play in perusing the texts of this brochure by one and all who have any interest in pure theistic achievements. The materialistic inspection often goes on to say that the provincial conception of theism has made the depicting of transcendental unity into diverse face quite opposed to the ethical consideration of the limited region. But we differ from such erroneous considerations when we get a prospective view of the manifested transcendentality eliminating all historicities and allegorical enterprises. All our enjoying mood should have a different direction when we take into account the transcendental entity who has obsessed all frailties and limitations of nature. So we solicit the happier mood of the scrutinizers to pay special attention to the importance of manifestive transcendence in Kṛṣṇa.

It was found necessary to publish this small book for the use of English-knowing people who are interested in the acme of transcendental truths in their manifestive phases. The theme delineated in the texts of this book is quite different from the ordinary heaps of poetical mundane literature, as they are confined to our limited aspiration of senses. The book was found in the South some four centuries ago and it is again brought into light in the very same country after a long time, just like the worshiping of the goddess Ganges by the offering of her own water.

Siddhānta Sarasvatī
Shree Gaudiya Math, Calcutta, the 1st August, 1932.

TEXT 1

ईश्वरः परमः कृष्णः सच्चिदानन्दविग्रहः ।
अनादिरादिर्गोविन्दः सर्वकारणकारणम् ॥१॥

īśvaraḥ paramaḥ kṛṣṇaḥ
sac-cid-ānanda-vigrahaḥ
anādir ādir govindaḥ
sarva-kāraṇa-kāraṇam

īśvaraḥ—the controller; *paramaḥ*—supreme; *kṛṣṇaḥ*—Lord Kṛṣṇa; *sat*—comprising eternal existence; *cit*—absolute knowledge; *ānanda*—and absolute bliss; *vigrahaḥ*—whose form; *anādiḥ*—without beginning; *ādiḥ*—the origin; *govindaḥ*—Lord Govinda; *sarva-kāraṇa-kāraṇam*—the cause of all causes.

Kṛṣṇa who is known as Govinda is the Supreme Godhead. He has an eternal blissful spiritual body. He is the origin of all. He has no other origin and He is the prime cause of all causes.

PURPORT

Kṛṣṇa is the exalted Supreme entity having His eternal name, eternal form, eternal attribution and eternal pastimes. The very name "Kṛṣṇa" implies His love-attracting designation, expressing by His eternal nomenclature the acme of entity. His eternal beautiful heavenly blue-tinged body glowing with the intensity of ever-existing knowledge has a flute in both His hands. As His inconceivable spiritual energy is all-extending, still He maintains His all-charming medium size by His qualifying spiritual instrumentals. His all-accommodating supreme subjectivity is nicely manifested in His eternal form. The concentrated all-time presence, uncovered knowledge and inebriating felicity have their beauty in Him. The mundane manifestive portion of His own Self is known as all-pervading Paramātmā, Īśvara (Superior Lord) or Viṣṇu (All-fostering). Hence it is evident that Kṛṣṇa is sole Supreme Godhead. His unrivaled or unique spiritual body of superexcellent charm is eternally unveiled with innumerable spiritual instrumentals (senses) and unreckonable attributes keeping their signifying location properly, adjusting at the same time by His inconceivable conciliative powers. This beautiful spiritual figure is identical with Kṛṣṇa and the spiritual entity of Kṛṣṇa is identical with His own figure.

The very intensely blended entity of eternal presence of felicitous cognition is the charming targeted holding or transcendental icon. It follows that the conception of the indistinguishable formless magnitude (Brahman) which is an indolent, lax, presentment of cognitive bliss, is merely a penumbra of intensely blended glow of the three concomitants, viz., the blissful, the substantive and the cognitive. This transcendental manifestive icon Kṛṣṇa in His original face is primordial background of magnitudinal infinite Brahman and of the all-pervasive oversoul. Kṛṣṇa as truly visioned in His variegated pastimes, such as owner of transcendental cows, chief of cowherds, consort of milkmaids, ruler of the terrestrial abode Gokula and object of worship by transcendental residents of Goloka beauties, is Govinda. He is the root cause of all causes who are the predominating and predominated agents of the universe. The glance of His projected fractional portion in the sacred originating water viz., the personal oversoul or Paramātmā, gives rise to a secondary potency—nature who creates this mundane universe. This oversoul's intermediate energy brings forth the individual souls analogously to the emanated rays of the sun.

This book is a treatise of Kṛṣṇa; so the preamble is enacted by chanting His name in the beginning.

TEXT 2

सहस्रपत्रकमलं गोकुलाख्यं महत्पदम् ।
तत्कर्णिकारं तद्धाम तदनन्तांशसम्भवम् ॥२॥

sahasra-patra-kamalaṁ
gokulākhyaṁ mahat padam
tat-karṇikāraṁ tad-dhāma
tad-anantāṁśa-sambhavam

sahasra-patra—possessing a thousand petals; *kamalam*—a lotus; *gokula-ākhyam*—known as Gokula; *mahat padam*—the superexcellent station; *tat*—of that (lotus); *karṇikāram*—the whorl; *tat*—of Him (Kṛṣṇa); *dhāma*—the abode; *tat*—that (Gokula); *ananta*—of His infinitary aspect, Balarāma; *aṁśa*—from a part; *sambhavam*—produced.

[The spiritual place of transcendental pastimes of Kṛṣṇa is portrayed in the second verse.] The superexcellent station of Kṛṣṇa, which is known as Gokula, has thousands of petals and a corolla like that of a lotus sprouted from a part of His infinitary aspect, the whorl of the leaves being the actual abode of Kṛṣṇa.

PURPORT

Gokula, like Goloka, is not a created mundane plane—unbounded character forms the display of His unlimited potency and His propagating manifestation. Baladeva is the mainstay of that energy. The transcendental entity of Baladeva has two aspects viz., infinite spiritual manifestation and infinite accommodating space for insentient gross things. The uniquadrantal delineation of material universe will be dealt with in the proper place. The triquadrantal extensions of the transcendental infinitary field of the almighty, unlamenting, nonperishing and nonapprehending unlimited situations of halo which are fully spiritual majestic foliation. This very majestical extension portrays the manifested lofty rich feature of the vaster unlimited region or greater atmosphere which has its resplendent location wholly beyond the realm of mundane nature, on the further shore of Virajā surrounded by the halo of Brahman or indistinguishable entity. This majestical power of unlimited spirit emanates on the upper portion of the luminous sphere into the most charming Gokula or eternally existing Goloka, exceedingly beautified by the assorted display of effulgence. Some designate this region as the abode of the Supreme Nārāyaṇa, or the original fountainhead. Hence Gokula, which is identical with Goloka, is the supreme plane. The same sphere shines as Goloka and Gokula respectively by its upper or transcendental and lower or mundane situation.

Śrī Sanātana Gosvāmī has told us as follows in his *Bṛhad-bhāgavatāmṛta* which embodies the final essence of all the books of instructions: "He displays His pastimes here in this land as He is used to do in Goloka. The difference between the two planes lies only in their locations as high and low; that is, in other words, Kṛṣṇa plays exactly the same part in Goloka as He exhibits on the mundane plane of Gokula. There is practically no difference between Gokula and Goloka save that this what exists in the shape of Goloka in the upper region is the same as Gokula on the mundane plane when Kṛṣṇa showed His various activity there. Śrī Jīva Gosvāmī has also inculcated the same in the *Bhagavat-sandarbha* of his 'Six Treatises.' To ascertain the plane of Goloka—Vṛndāvana is the eternal abode of Kṛṣṇa and Goloka and Vṛndāvana are identically one, and though both are identical, yet Kṛṣṇa's inconceivable energy has made Goloka the acme of this spiritual kingdom and Gokula of Mathurā province forming a part of the mundane plane which is also a manifestation of triquadrantal *vibhūti* (conducting majesty). Poor human understanding cannot possibly make out how the extensive triquadrantal, which is beyond human comprehension, can be accommodated in the limited nether material universe of a uniquadrantal disclosure. Gokula is a spiritual plane, hence his condescended position in the region of material space, time, etc., is in no way restricted but unlimitedly manifested with his full boundless propriety. But conditioned souls are apt to assert a material conception in regard to Gokula by their miserable senses so as to bring him below the level of their intellect. Though the eye of an observer is impeded by a cloud when gazing at the sun and though the tiny cloud can never really cover the sun, still the clouded vision apparently observes the sun as covered by the cloud. In just the same way the conditioned souls with their obscured intelligence, senses and decisions, accept Gokula as a piece of measurable land. We can see Gokula from Goloka which is eternal. This is also a mystery. The attainment of final beatitude is the success in attaining one's eternal self. The success in identifying the true self is finally achieved when the screen of gross and subtle coils of conditioned souls is removed by the sweet will of Kṛṣṇa. However, the idea of Goloka is seen to differ from Gokula till the success in unalloyed devotion is achieved. The transcendental plane of infinite spiritual manifestation having thousands of petals and corolla like those of the lotus, is Gokula, the eternal abode of Kṛṣṇa.

TEXT 3

कर्णिकारं महद्यन्त्रं षट्कोणं वज्रकीलकम् ।
षडङ्गषट्पदीस्थानं प्रकृत्या पुरुषेण च ॥
प्रेमानन्दमहानन्दरसेनावस्थितं हि यत् ।
ज्योतीरूपेण मनुना कामबीजेन सङ्गतम् ॥३॥

karṇikāraṁ mahad yantraṁ
ṣaṭ-koṇaṁ vajra-kīlakam
ṣaḍ-aṅga-ṣaṭ-padī-sthānaṁ
prakṛtyā puruṣeṇa ca

premānanda-mahānanda-
rasenāvasthitaṁ hi yat
jyotī-rūpeṇa manunā
kāma-bījena saṅgatam

karṇikāram—the whorl; *mahat*—great; *yantram*—figure; *ṣaṭ-koṇam*—a hexagon; *vajra*—like a diamond; *kīlakam*—the central support; *ṣaṭ-aṅga-ṣaṭ-padī*—of the eighteen-syllable *mantra* with sixfold divisions; *sthānam*—the place of manifestation; *prakṛtyā*—along with the predominated aspect of the Absolute; *puruṣeṇa*—along with the predominating aspect of the Absolute; *ca*—also; *prema-ānanda*—of the bliss of love of God; *mahā-ānanda*—of the great transcendental jubilations; *rasena*—with the *rasa* (mellow); *avasthitam*—situated; *hi*—certainly; *yat*—which; *jyotiḥ-rūpeṇa*—transcendental; *manunā*—with the *mantra; kāma-bījena*—with the *kāma-bīja* (*klīṁ*); *saṅgatam*—joined.

The whorl of that transcendental lotus is the realm wherein dwells Kṛṣṇa. It is a hexagonal figure, the abode of the indwelling predominated and predominating aspect of the Absolute. Like a diamond the central supporting figure of self-luminous Kṛṣṇa stands as the transcendental source of all potencies. The holy name consisting of eighteen transcendental letters is manifested in a hexagonal figure with sixfold divisions.

PURPORT

The transcendental pastimes of Kṛṣṇa are twofold, viz., manifested and nonmanifested. The pastimes in Vṛndāvana visible to mortal eyes are the manifestive *līlā* of Śrī Kṛṣṇa, and that which is not so visible, is nonmanifestive *līlā* of Kṛṣṇa. The nonmanifestive *līlā* is always visible in Goloka and the same is visible to human eyes in Gokula, if Kṛṣṇa so desires. In his *Kṛṣṇa-sandarbha* Śrī Jīva Gosvāmī Prabhu says, "Nonmanifestive pastimes are expressed in manifestive *kṛṣṇa-līlā*, and *goloka-līlā* is the nonmanifestive pastimes of Kṛṣṇa visualized from the mundane plane." This is also corroborated by Śrī Rūpa in his *Bhāgavatāmṛta*. The progressive transcendental manifestation of Gokula is Goloka. So Goloka is the selfsame majestic manifestation of Gokula. The eternal pastimes of Śrī Kṛṣṇa, although not visible in Gokula, are eternally manifested in Goloka. Goloka is the transcendental majestic manifestation of Gokula. The manifestations of the nonmanifestive pastimes of Kṛṣṇa with regard to the conditioned souls, are twofold, viz., (1) worship through the channel of the *mantras* (inaudibly recited, liberating, self-dedicatory, transcendental sounds), (2) spontaneous outflow of heart's spiritual love for Kṛṣṇa. Śrī Jīva Gosvāmī has said that worship through the *mantra* is possible permanently in the proper place, when confined to one pastime. This meditative manifestation of Goloka is the pastime attended with the worship of Kṛṣṇa through the *mantra*. Again, the pastimes that are performed in different planes and in different moods, are autocratic in diverse ways; hence *svā-rasikī*, i.e., spontaneous, outflow of heart's spiritual love for Kṛṣṇa. This *śloka* conveys a twofold meaning. One meaning is that in the pastime attended with worship through the *mantra* consisting of eighteen transcendental letters, transcendental words contained in the said *mantra* being differently placed make a manifestation of only one *līlā* of Śrī Kṛṣṇa. As for example *klīṁ kṛṣṇāya govindāya gopījana-vallabhāya svāhā*—this is a hexagonal *mantra* consisting of six transcendental words, viz., (1) *kṛṣṇāya*, (2) *govindāya*, (3) *gopījana*, (4) *vallabhāya*, (5) *svā*, (6) *hā*. These six transcendental words, when placed juxtapositionally, indicate the *mantra*.

The hexagonal great transcendental machinery is in this wise.

The principal seed, i.e. *klīṁ*, is situated in the instrument as the central pivot. Anybody with an impression of such an instrument in his mind and concentrating his thought on such spiritual entities, can attain, like Candradhvaja, to the knowledge of the cognitive principle. The word *svā* indicates *kṣetrajña* i.e., one who is conversant with one's inner self, and the word *hā* indicates the transcendental nature. This meaning of the *mantra* has also been corroborated by *Śrī Hari-bhakti-vilāsa*. The general meaning is this that one who is desirous of entering into the esoteric pastimes of Kṛṣṇa will have to practice His transcendental service along with the culture of the devotional knowledge relative to Him. (1) *kṛṣṇa-svarūpa*—the proper Self of Kṛṣṇa; (2) *kṛṣṇasya cin-maya-vraja-līlā-vilāsa-svarūpa*—the true nature of Kṛṣṇa's transcendental pastimes in Vraja; (3) *tat-parikara-gopījana-svarūpa*—the true nature of His spiritual associates in Vraja, viz., the spiritual milkmen and the milkmaids; (4) *tad-vallabha*—the true nature of self-surrender to Kṛṣṇa in the footsteps of the spiritual milkmaids of Vraja; (5) *śuddha-jīvasya cid-(jñāna)-svarūpa*—the true nature of the spiritual knowledge of the unalloyed individual soul; (6) *cit-prakṛtir arthāt kṛṣṇa-sevā-svabhāva*—the true nature of transcendental service to Kṛṣṇa is this that the esoteric relation is established on the awakening of one's pure cognition. The meaning is that *rasa* is only the transcendental service of the central refuge Śrī Kṛṣṇa, as predominating aspect of the Absolute, by one's ego as the spiritual maid of the predominated moiety of the absolute integer, attended with pure devotion in the shape of one's entire self-surrender. The pastime in Goloka or in Gokula during the stage of devotional progress, is the meditative worship through the *mantra*, and during the stage of perfection the pastimes manifest themselves as the unrestrained transcendental jubilations. This is the real aspect of Goloka or Gokula, which will be made more explicit in due course. The meaning of the words *jyotī-rūpeṇa manunā* is that the transcendental meaning is expressed in the *mantra* by means of which, on transcendental desire of love for Kṛṣṇa and the service of Kṛṣṇa being added, one is established in the eternal love of Kṛṣṇa. Such eternal pastimes are eternally manifested in Goloka.

TEXT 4

तत्किञ्जल्कं तदंशानां तत्पत्राणि श्रियामपि ॥४॥

tat-kiñjalkaṁ tad-aṁśānāṁ
tat-patrāṇi śriyām api

tat—of that (lotus); *kiñjalkam*—the petals; *tat-aṁśānām*—of His (Kṛṣṇa's) fragmental portions; *tat*—of that (lotus); *patrāṇi*—the leaves; *śriyām*—of the *gopīs* (headed by Śrīmatī Rādhārāṇī); *api*—also.

The whorl of that eternal realm Gokula is the hexagonal abode of Kṛṣṇa. Its petals are the abodes of gopīs who are part and parcel of Kṛṣṇa to whom they are most lovingly devoted and are similar in essence. The petals shine beautifully like so many walls. The extended leaves of that lotus are the gardenlike dhāma, i.e. spiritual abode of Śrī Rādhikā, the most beloved of Kṛṣṇa.

PURPORT

The transcendental Gokula is shaped like the lotus. The eternal world is like a hexagonal figure; in that the entities Śrī Rādhā-Kṛṣṇa, appearing in the form of a *mantra* consisting of eighteen transcendental letters, are centered. The propagating manifestations emanating from the *cit* potency are present there with the said entities as the center. Śrī Rādhā-Kṛṣṇa is the primary cause or the seed Himself. *Gopāla-tāpanī* says, "*Oṁkāra*" signifies the All-Powerful Gopāla and His potency; and "*klīṁ*" is the same as *oṁkāra*. Hence *kāma-bīja* or the primary cause of all-love, is connotative of the entities Śrī Rādhā-Kṛṣṇa.

TEXT 5

चतुरस्रं तत्परितः श्वेतद्वीपाख्यमद्भुतम् ।
चतुरस्रं चतुर्मूर्तेश्चतुर्धाम चतुष्कृतम् ॥
चतुर्भिः पुरुषार्थैश्च चतुर्भिर्हेतुभिर्वृतम् ।
शूलैर्दशभिरानद्धमूर्ध्वाधो दिग्विदिक्ष्वपि ॥
अष्टभिर्निधिभिर्जुष्टमष्टभिः सिद्धिभिस्तथा ।
मनुरूपैश्च दशभिर्दिक्पालैः परितो वृतम् ॥
श्यामैर्गौरैश्च रक्तैश्च शुक्लैश्च पार्षदर्षभैः ।
शोभितं शक्तिभिस्ताभिरद्भुताभिः समन्ततः ॥५॥

catur-asraṁ tat-paritaḥ
śvetadvīpākhyam adbhutam
catur-asraṁ catur-mūrteś
catur-dhāma catuṣ-kṛtam

caturbhiḥ puruṣārthaiś ca
caturbhir hetubhir vṛtam
śūlair daśabhir ānaddham
ūrdhvādho dig-vidikṣv api

aṣṭabhir nidhibhir juṣṭam
aṣṭabhiḥ siddhibhis tathā
manu-rūpaiś ca daśabhir
dik-pālaiḥ parito vṛtam

śyāmair gauraiś ca raktaiś ca
śuklaiś ca pārṣadarṣabhaiḥ
śobhitaṁ śaktibhis tābhir
adbhutābhiḥ samantataḥ

catuḥ-asram—quadrangular place; *tat*—that (Gokula); *paritaḥ*—surrounding; *śveta-dvīpa*—Śvetadvīpa (the white island); *ākhyam*—named; *adbhutam*—mysterious; *catuḥ-asram*—quadrangular; *catuḥ-mūrteḥ*—of the four primary expansions (Vāsudeva, Saṅkarṣaṇa, Pradyumna and Aniruddha); *catuḥ-dhāma*—consisting of four abodes; *catuḥ-kṛtam*—divided into four parts; *caturbhiḥ*—by the four; *puruṣa-arthaiḥ*—human requirements; *ca*—and; *caturbhiḥ*—by the four; *hetubhiḥ*—causes, or bases of achievement; *vṛtam*—enveloped; *śūlaiḥ*—with tridents; *daśabhiḥ*—ten; *ānaddham*—fixed; *ūrdhva-adhaḥ*—upwards and downwards (the zenith and nadir); *dik*—(in) the directions (north, south, east, and west); *vidikṣu*—and in the intermediate directions (northeast, southeast, southwest, and northwest); *api*—also; *aṣṭabhiḥ*—with the eight; *nidhibhiḥ*—jewels; *juṣṭam*—endowed; *aṣṭabhiḥ*—with the eight; *siddhibhiḥ*—mystic perfections (*aṇimā*, *laghimā*, *prāpti*, *prākāmya*, *mahimā*, *īśitva*, *vaśitva*, and *kāmāvasāyitā*); *tathā*—also; *manu-rūpaiḥ*—in the form of *mantras; ca*—and; *daśabhiḥ*—by ten; *dik-pālaiḥ*—protectors of the directions; *paritaḥ*—all around; *vṛtam*—surrounded; *śyāmaiḥ*—blue; *gauraiḥ*—yellow; *ca*—and; *raktaiḥ*—red; *ca*—and; *śuklaiḥ*—white; *ca*—also; *pārṣada-ṛṣabhaiḥ*—with the topmost associates; *śobhitam*—shining; *śaktibhiḥ*—with potencies; *tābhiḥ*—those; *adbhutābhiḥ*—extraordinary; *samantataḥ*—on all sides.

[The surrounding external plane of Gokula is described in this verse.] There is a mysterious quadrangular place named Śvetadvīpa surrounding the outskirts of Gokula. Śvetadvīpa is divided into four parts on all sides. The abode of Vāsudeva, Saṅkarṣaṇa, Pradyumna and Aniruddha are separately located in each of these four parts. These four divided abodes are enveloped by the fourfold human requirements such as piety, wealth, passion and liberation, as also by the four Vedas, viz., Ṛg, Sāma, Yajur and

Atharva, which deal with the mantra and which are the bases of achievements of the fourfold mundane requirements. Ten tridents are fixed in the ten directions, including the zenith and nadir. The eight directions are decorated with the eight jewels of Mahāpadma, Padma, Śaṅkha, Makara, Kacchapa, Mukunda, Kunda, and Nīla. There are ten protectors [dik-pālas] of the ten directions in the form of mantra. The associates of the hues of blue, yellow, red and white and the extraordinary potencies bearing the names of Vimala, etc., shine on all sides.

PURPORT

Primarily Gokula is the seat of transcendental love and devotion. Hence Yamunā, Śrī Govardhana, Śrī Rādhā-kuṇḍa, etc., of the terrestrial Vraja-maṇḍala lie within Gokula. Again, all the majesties of Vaikuṇṭha are manifested there extending in all directions. The pastimes of the four propagating manifestations are all there in their proper places. The *paravyoma* Vaikuṇṭha has got its extension from the display of the four propagating manifestations. Salvation as of Vaikuṇṭha, and piety, wealth and passion pertaining to worldly people, are in the proper places in Gokula as their original seed, i.e., primary cause. The *Vedas* also are engaged in singing the song of the Lord of Gokula. There are ten tridents in ten directions to prevent and disappoint those who are aspirants for having an entrance into Goloka through meditations without the grace of Kṛṣṇa. Self-conceited people who try to reach this region through the paths of *yoga* (meditation) and *jñāna* (empiric knowledge) are baffled in their attempts, being pierced by the ten tridents. Self-annihilation has its excellence in Brahma-dhāma which represents the outside covering of Goloka in the shape of tridents. *Śūla* means a trident; the mundane threefold attributes and the threefold divisions of time represent the trident. *Aṣṭāṅga-yogīs* i.e. ascetics who practice the eightfold *yoga*, are the nondifferentiative liberationists who, trying to approach in the direction of Goloka, fall headlong into the pits of disappointment by being pierced and cut asunder by these tridents placed in ten directions. Those who proceed towards the direction of Goloka through the channel of devotion alloyed with majestic ideas, are fascinated with the charms of Vaikuṇṭha which is the outer covering plane of Śrī Goloka, at the sight of the eight perfections, viz., *aṇimā*, etc., and majesties like *mahāpadma*, etc. Those who are less forward in their intelligence relapse to the sevenfold world falling under the control of the ten protectors (of the ten directions) in the guise of *mantras*. In this wise, Goloka has become unknowable and inaccessible. It is only the divine selves of Godhead, the propounders of the divine dispensations for the different ages, who are always forward there to favor the approaching devotees who seek entry into the realm of Goloka through the channel of pure devotional love. These divine forms of Godhead are surrounded there with attendants of their respective natures. Śvetadvīpa in Goloka is their place of abode. Hence Śrīla Ṭhākura Vṛndāvana the manifest Vyāsa of *caitanya-līlā*, has described the village of Navadvīpa as bearing the name of Śvetadvīpa. In this Śvetadvīpa the concluding portions of the pastimes of Gokula exist eternally as the pastimes of Navadvīpa. Hence the region of Navadvīpa, Vraja and the realm of Goloka are one and the same indivisible entity; the difference only lies in the manifestations of the infinite variety of sentiments, corresponding to the diverse nature of their devotional love. There is in this a most hidden principle which only the greatest souls who are possessed of the highest transcendental love, are enabled to realize by the direct grace of Kṛṣṇa. The truth is as follows: In this mundane world there are fourteen spheres disposed in the graded order of high and low. Persons living with wives and children hankering for the pleasure-giving effect of their fruitive actions, move up and down within the limits of the three worlds of Bhūḥ, Bhuvaḥ and Svaḥ. *Brahmacārīs* of great austerities, ascetics and persons addicted to hypothetical truth, persons of a neutral disposition adopting nonfruitive works by an aptitude which seeks to be free from all mundane desires, move up and down within the limits of the worlds of Mahaḥ, Janaḥ, Tapaḥ and Satya. Above these worlds lies the abode of four-headed Brahmā, above which lies the unlimited realm of Vaikuṇṭha of Viṣṇu, Kṣīrodakaśāyī, lying in the ocean of milk. *Paramahaṁsa-sannyāsīs* and the demons killed by Śrī Hari, by crossing the Virajā, i.e., by passing beyond the fourteen worlds, enter into the luminous realm of Brahman and attain to *nirvāṇa* in the form of temporary abeyance of the temporal ego. But the devotee actuated by knowledge (*jñāna-bhakta*), the devotee actuated by the pure devotional aptitude (*śuddha-bhakta*), the devotee imbued with loving devotion (*prema-bhakta*), the devotee actuated by pure love (*premapara-bhakta*), and the devotee impelled by overwhelming love (*premātura-bhakta*), who serve the majesty of Godhead, have their locations in Vaikuṇṭha, i.e., the transcendental realm of Śrī Nārāyaṇa.

The devotees who are imbued with all-love and who walk in the footsteps of the spiritual maids of Vraja, alone attain to the realm of Goloka. The different locations of the devotees in Goloka according to the respective differences in the nature of their *rasa*, i.e., mellow quality, are settled by the inconceivable power of Kṛṣṇa. The pure devotees following the devotees of Vraja and those following the pure devotees of Navadvīpa are located in the realm of Kṛṣṇa and Gaura respectively. The identical devotees of Vraja and Navadvīpa simultaneously attain to the pleasures of service in the realm of Kṛṣṇa and Gaura. Śrī Jīva Gosvāmī writes in his work *Gopāla-campū* that "the supreme transcendental realm is called Goloka being the abode of *go*, transcendental cows, and *gopa*, transcendental cowherds. This is the seat of the *rasa* pastimes of the absolute Śrī Kṛṣṇa. Again the realm is called Śvetadvīpa owing to the realization of some of the *rasas* which are the inconceivable manifestation derived from the untouched purity of that supreme realm. The twofold entities of the supreme Goloka and the supreme Śvetadvīpa are indivisibly the realm of Goloka." The gist of the whole matter is this—Goloka as Śvetadvīpa is eternally manifest because the pleasures of enjoyment of the *rasa* could not be had in its entirety in the pastimes of Kṛṣṇa in Vraja. He accepts the emotion and effulgence of His predominated moiety, Śrī Rādhikā, and makes an eternal pastime for the enjoyment of *kṛṣṇa-rasa* there. Śrī Kṛṣṇacandra coveting to taste the following pleasures, viz., to realize (1) the nature of the greatness of love of Śrī Rādhā; (2) the nature of the wonderful sweetness of His love of which Śrī Rādhikā has got the taste; (3) the nature of the exquisite joy that accrues to Śrī Rādhā by Her realization of the sweetness of His love, took His birth, like the moon, in the ocean of the womb of Śrī Śacī-devī. The esoteric desire of Śrī Jīva Gosvāmī Prabhu is herein made manifest. In the *Veda* it is also said, "Let me tell you the mystery. In Navadvīpa, the identical realm of Goloka, on the bank of the Ganges, Gauracandra who is Govinda, the entity of pure cognition, who has two hands, who is the soul of all souls, who has the supreme great personality as the great meditative *sannyāsin* and who is beyond the threefold mundane attributes, makes the process of pure unalloyed devotion manifest in this mundane world. He is sole Godhead. He is the source of all forms, the Supreme Soul and is Godhead manifesting Himself in yellow, red, blue and white colors. He is the direct entity of pure cognition full of the spiritual (*cit*) potency. He is the figure of the devotee. He is the bestower of devotion and cognizable by devotion alone. The selfsame Gauracandra, who is no other than Kṛṣṇa Himself, in order to taste the *rasa* of the pastimes of Rādhā-Kṛṣṇa in Goloka, is manifest in the eternal realm of Navadvīpa identical with Goloka." This is also clear from the Vedic declarations, viz., *āsan varṇās trayaḥ*, *kṛṣṇa-varṇaṁ tviṣākṛṣṇam*, *yathā paśyaḥ paśyati rukma-varṇam*, *mahān prabhur vai* and various other statements of the theistic scriptures. Just as Śrī Kṛṣṇa had His birth in the mundane Gokula through the agency of Yogamāyā who is the primal energy of the Supreme Lord, so with her help He manifests the *līlā* of His birth in the womb of Śacī-devī in Navadvīpa on this mundane plane. These are the absolute truths of spiritual science and not the outcome of imaginary speculation under the thraldom of the deluding energy of Godhead.

TEXT 6

एवं ज्योतिर्मयो देवः सदानन्दः परात्परः ।
आत्मारामस्य तस्यास्ति प्रकृत्या न समागमः ॥६॥

evaṁ jyotir-mayo devaḥ
sad-ānandaḥ parāt paraḥ
ātmārāmasya tasyāsti
prakṛtyā na samāgamaḥ

evam—thus; *jyotiḥ-mayaḥ*—transcendental; *devaḥ*—the Lord; *sat-ānandaḥ*—the own Self of eternal ecstasies; *parāt paraḥ*—the superior of all superiors; *ātma-ārāmasya*—engaged in the enjoyments of the transcendental realm; *tasya*—of Him; *asti*—there is; *prakṛtyā*—with the mundane potency; *na*—not; *samāgamaḥ*—association.

The Lord of Gokula is the transcendental Supreme Godhead, the own Self of eternal ecstasies. He is the superior of all superiors and is busily engaged in the enjoyments of the transcendental realm and has no association with His mundane potency.

PURPORT

The sole potency of Kṛṣṇa which is spiritual, functioning as Kṛṣṇa's own proper power, has manifested His pastimes of Goloka or Gokula. By her grace individual souls who are constituents of the marginal potency can have admission into even those pastimes. The deluding energy, who is of the nature of the perverted reflection of the spiritual (*cit*) potency, has got her location on the other side of the river Virajā, which surrounds the Brahma-dhāma forming the boundary of Mahā-Vaikuṇṭha as the outer envelope of Goloka. The position of Goloka being absolutely unalloyed with the mundane, deluding energy, far from having any association with Kṛṣṇa, feels ashamed to appear before His view.

TEXT 7

ममाययारममाणस्य न वियोगस्तया सह ।
आत्मना रमया रेमे त्यक्तकालं सिसृक्षया ॥७॥

māyayāramamāṇasya
na viyogas tayā saha
ātmanā ramayā reme
tyakta-kālaṁ sisṛkṣayā

māyayā—with the illusory energy; *aramamāṇasya*—of Him, who never consorts; *na*—not; *viyogaḥ*—complete separation; *tayā*—her; *saha*—from; *ātmanā*—with His own; *ramayā*—spiritual potency, Ramā; *reme*—consorts; *tyakta-kālam*—by casting His glance in the shape of sending His time energy; *sisṛkṣayā*—with the desire to create.

Kṛṣṇa never consorts with His illusory energy. Still her connection is not entirely cut off from the Absolute Truth. When He intends to create the material world the amorous pastime, in which He engages by consorting with His own spiritual [cit] potency Ramā by casting His glance at the deluding energy in the shape of sending His time energy, is an auxiliary activity.

PURPORT

The illusory energy has no direct contact with Kṛṣṇa, but has got indirect contact. Viṣṇu the prime cause, lying in the Causal

Ocean, the plenary portion of Mahā-Saṅkarṣaṇa who has His seat in Mahā-Vaikuṇṭha the sphere of Kṛṣṇa's own extended transcendental pastimes, casts His glance towards the deluding energy. Even in casting His glance He has no contact with the deluding energy because the spiritual (*cit*) potency Ramā then carries the function of His glance as His unpolluted ever-submissive potency. The deluding energy as the maidservant of the spiritual (*cit*) potency Ramā, serves the manifested plenary portion of Godhead consorted with Ramā, the time energy representing the force of activity and instrumentality of Ramā; hence there is found the process of masculinity or the creative force.

TEXT 8

नियतिः सा रमा देवी तत्प्रिया तद्वशं तदा ।
तल्लिङ्गं भगवान् शम्भुर्ज्योतिरूपः सनातनः ।
या योनिः सापरा शक्तिः कामो बीजं महद्धरेः ॥८॥

niyatiḥ sā ramā devī
tat-priyā tad-vaśaṁ tadā
tal-liṅgaṁ bhagavān śambhur
jyotī-rūpaḥ sanātanaḥ
yā yoniḥ sāparā śaktiḥ
kāmo bījaṁ mahad dhareḥ

niyatiḥ—the regulator; *sā*—she; *ramā*—the spiritual potency; *devī*—the goddess; *tat*—of Him; *priyā*—beloved; *tat*—of Him; *vaśam*—under the control; *tadā*—then (at the time of creation); *tat*—of Him; *liṅgam*—the masculine symbol, or manifested emblem; *bhagavān*—possessing opulences; *śambhuḥ*—Śambhu; *jyotiḥ-rūpaḥ*—halo; *sanātanaḥ*—eternal; *yā*—which; *yoniḥ*—the symbol of mundane feminine productivity; *sā*—that; *aparā*—nonabsolute; *śaktiḥ*—potency; *kāmaḥ*—the desire; *bījam*—the seed; *mahat*—the faculty of perverted cognition; *hareḥ*—of the Supreme Lord.

[The secondary process of association with Māyā is described.] Ramādevī, the spiritual [cit] potency, beloved consort of the Supreme Lord, is the regulatrix of all entities. The divine plenary portion of Kṛṣṇa creates the mundane world. At creation there appears a divine halo of the nature of His own subjective portion [svāṁśa]. This halo is divine Śambhu, the masculine symbol or manifested emblem of the Supreme Lord. This halo is the dim twilight reflection of the supreme eternal effulgence. This masculine symbol is the subjective portion of divinity who functions as progenitor of the mundane world, subject to the supreme regulatrix [niyati]. The conceiving potency in regard to mundane creation makes her appearance out of the supreme regulatrix. She is Māyā, the limited, nonabsolute [aparā] potency, the symbol of mundane feminine productivity. The intercourse of these two brings forth the faculty of perverted cognition, the reflection of the seed of the procreative desire of the Supreme Lord.

PURPORT

Saṅkarṣaṇa possessed of creative desire is the subjective portion of Kṛṣṇa taking the initiative in bringing about the birth of the mundane world. Lying in the causal water as the primal *puruṣa-avatāra* He casts His glance towards Māyā (the limited potency). Such glance is the efficient cause of the mundane creation. Śambhu the symbol of masculine mundane procreation is the dim halo of this reflected effulgence. It is this symbol which is applied to the organ of generation of Māyā, the shadow of Ramā or the divine potency. The first phase of the appearance of the mundane desire created by Mahā-Viṣṇu is called the seminal principle of *mahat* or the perverted cognitive faculty. It is this which is identical with the mental principle ripe for procreative activity. The conception underlying it is that it is the will of the *puruṣa* who creates by using the efficient and material principles. Efficiency is Māyā or the productive feminine organ. The material principle is Śambhu or the procreative masculine organ. Mahā-Viṣṇu is *puruṣa* or the dominating divine person wielding the will. *Pradhāna* or the substantive principle in the shape of mundane entities, is the material principle. Nature embodying the accommodating principle (*ādhāra*), is Māyā. The principle of embodied will bringing about the intercourse of the two, is the dominating divine person (*puruṣa*), subjective portion of Kṛṣṇa, the manifestor of the mundane world. All of these three are creators. The seed of amorous creative desire in Goloka, is the embodiment of pure cognition. The seed of sex desire to be found in this mundane world, is that of Kālī, etc., who are the shadows of the divine potency. The former, although it is the prototype of the latter, is located very far from it. The seed of the mundane sex desire is the perverted reflection in this mundane world of the seed of the original creative desire. The process of the appearance of Śambhu is recorded in the tenth and fifteenth *ślokas*.

TEXT 9

लिङ्गयोन्यात्मिका जाता इमा माहेश्वरीप्रजाः ॥९॥

liṅga-yony-ātmikā jātā
imā māheśvarī-prajāḥ

liṅga—of the mundane masculine generative organs; *yoni*—and of the mundane feminine generative organs; *ātmikāḥ*—as the embodiment; *jātāḥ*—born; *imāḥ*—these; *māheśvarī*—of the consort of the great lord of this mundane world; *prajāḥ*—the offspring.

All offspring of the consort of the great lord [Maheśvara] of this mundane world are of the nature of the embodiment of the mundane masculine and feminine generative organs.

PURPORT

The full quadrantal extension of the Supreme Lord, is His majesty. Of this the triquadrantal extensions of unlamenting, nonperishing and nonapprehending situations constitute the majesties of the realms of Vaikuṇṭha and Goloka, etc. In this temporal realm of Māyā *devas* and men, etc.—all these together with all mundane worlds—are the great majesties of the limited potency. All these entities are embodiments of the masculine and feminine organs of generation by the distinction of efficient and material causal principles; or, in other words, they are produced by the process of sexual intercourse between the male and female organs of generation. All the information that has been accumulated by the agency of the sciences of this world, possesses this nature of sexual co-union. Trees, plants and even all insentient entities are embodiments of the co-union of male and female. The feature that is of special significance is that although such expressions as "the generative organs of male and female" are indecorous yet in scientific literature these words, expressing the above-mentioned principles, are exceedingly wholesome and productive of abiding value. Indecorum is merely an entity pertaining to the external custom of society. But science, and specially the highest science, cannot destroy the true entity by deference to social custom. Wherefore, in order to demonstrate the seed of mundane sex desire, the basic principle of this phenomenal world, the use of those identical words is indispensable. By the use of all these words only the masculine energy or the predominating active potency, and female energy or the predominated active potency, are to be understood.

TEXT 10

शक्तिमान् पुरुषः सोऽयं लिङ्गरूपी महेश्वरः ।
तस्मिन्न् आविरभूल्लिङ्गे महाविष्णुर्जगत्पतिः ॥१०॥

śaktimān puruṣaḥ so 'yaṁ
liṅga-rūpī maheśvaraḥ
tasminn āvirabhūl liṅge
mahā-viṣṇur jagat-patiḥ

śaktimān—joined to his female consort; *puruṣaḥ*—person; *saḥ*—he; *ayam*—this; *liṅga-rūpī*—in the form of the male generating organ; *mahā-īśvaraḥ*—Śambhu, the lord of this mundane world; *tasmin*—in that; *āvirabhūt*—manifested; *liṅge*—in the manifested emblem; *mahā-viṣṇuḥ*—Mahā-Viṣṇu; *jagat-patiḥ*—the Lord of the world.

The person embodying the material causal principle, viz., the great lord of this mundane world [Maheśvara] Śamhhu, in the form of the male generating organ, is joined to his female consort the limited energy [Māyā] as the efficient causal principle. The Lord of the world Mahā-Viṣṇu is manifest in him by His subjective portion in the form of His glance.

PURPORT

In the transcendental atmosphere (*para-vyoma*), where spiritual majesty preponderates, there is present Śrī Nārāyaṇa who is not different from Kṛṣṇa. Mahā-Saṅkarṣaṇa, subjective plenary facsimile of the extended personality of Śrī Nārāyaṇa, is also the divine plenary portion of the propagatory embodiment of Śrī Kṛṣṇa. By the power of His spiritual energy a plenary subjective portion of Him, eternally reposing in the neutral stream of Virajā forming the boundary between the spiritual and mundane realms, casts His glance, at creation, unto the limited shadow potency. Māyā, who is located far away from Himself. Thereupon Śambhu, lord of *pradhāna* embodying the substantive principle of all material entities, who is the same as Rudra, the dim reflection of the Supreme Lord's own divine glance, consummates his intercourse with Māyā, the efficient mundane causal principle. But he can do nothing independently of the energy of Mahā-Viṣṇu representing the direct spiritual power of Kṛṣṇa. Therefore, the principle of *mahat*, or the perverted cognitive faculty, is produced only when the subjective plenary portion of Kṛṣṇa, viz., the prime divine *avatāra* Mahā-Viṣṇu who is the subjective portion of Saṅkarṣaṇa, Himself the subjective portion of Kṛṣṇa, is propitious towards the active mutual endeavors of Māyā, Śiva's consort (*śakti*), and *pradhāna* or the principle of substantive mundane causality. Agreeably to the initiative of Mahā-Viṣṇu the consort of Śiva creates successively the mundane ego (*ahaṅkāra*), the five mundane elements (*bhūtas*) viz., space etc., their attributes (*tan-mātras*) and the limited senses of the conditioned soul (*jīva*). The constituent particles, in the form of pencils of effulgence of Mahā-Viṣṇu, are manifest as the individual souls (*jīvas*). This will be elaborated in the sequel.

TEXT 11

सहस्रशीर्षा पुरुषः सहस्राक्षः सहस्रपात् ।
सहस्रबाहुर्विश्वात्मा सहस्रांशः सहस्रसूः ॥११॥

sahasra-śīrṣā puruṣaḥ
sahasrākṣaḥ sahasra-pāt
sahasra-bāhur viśvātmā
sahasrāṁśaḥ sahasra-sūḥ

sahasra-śīrṣā—possessing thousands of heads; *puruṣaḥ*—Lord Mahā-Viṣṇu, the first *puruṣa-avatāra; sahasra-akṣaḥ*—possessing thousands of eyes; *sahasra-pāt*—possessing thousands of legs; *sahasra-bāhuḥ*—possessing thousands of arms; *viśva-ātmā*—the Supersoul of the universe; *sahasra-aṁśaḥ*—the source of thousands of *avatāras; sahasra-sūḥ*—the creator of thousands of individual souls.

The Lord of the mundane world, Mahā-Viṣṇu, possesses thousands of thousands of heads, eyes, hands. He is the source of thousands of thousands of avatāras in His thousands of thousands of subjective portions. He is the creator of thousands of thousands of individual souls.

PURPORT

Mahā-Viṣṇu, the object of worship of the hymns of all the *Vedas*, is possessed of an infinity of senses and potencies, and He is the prime *avatāra-puruṣa*, the source of all the *avatāras*.

TEXT 12

नारायणः स भगवान् आपस्तस्मात्सनातनात् ।
आविरासीत्कारणार्णो निधिः सङ्कर्षणात्मकः ।
योगनिद्रां गतस्तस्मिन् सहस्रांशः स्वयं महान् ॥१२॥

nārāyaṇaḥ sa bhagavān
āpas tasmāt sanātanāt
āvirāsīt kāraṇārṇo
nidhiḥ saṅkarṣaṇātmakaḥ
yoga-nidrāṁ gatas tasmin
sahasrāṁśaḥ svayaṁ mahān

nārāyaṇaḥ—named Nārāyaṇa; *saḥ*—that; *bhagavān*—Supreme Personality of Godhead, Mahā-Viṣṇu; *āpaḥ*—water; *tasmāt*—from that; *sanātanāt*—eternal person; *āvirāsīt*—has sprung; *kāraṇa-arṇaḥ*—the Causal Ocean; *nidhiḥ*—expanse of water; *saṅkarṣaṇa-ātmakaḥ*—the subjective portion of Saṅkarṣaṇa; *yoga-nidrām gataḥ*—in the state of deep sleep; *tasmin*—in that (water); *sahasra-aṁśaḥ*—with thousands of portions; *svayam*—Himself; *mahān*—the Supreme Person.

The same Mahā-Viṣṇu is spoken of by the name of "Nārāyaṇa" in this mundane world. From that eternal person has sprung the vast expanse of water of the spiritual Causal Ocean. The subjective portion of Saṅkarṣaṇa who abides in paravyoma, the above supreme puruṣa with thousands of subjective portions, reposes in the state of divine sleep [yoga-nidrā] in the waters of the spiritual Causal Ocean.

PURPORT

Yoga-nidrā (divine sleep) is spoken of as ecstatic trance which is of the nature of the bliss of the true subjective personality. The above-mentioned Ramādevī is *yoga-nidrā* in the form of Yogamāyā.

TEXT 13

तद्रोमबिल जालेषु बीजं सङ्कर्षणस्य च ।
हैमान्यण्डानि जातानि महाभूतावृतानि तु ॥१३॥

tad-roma-bila jāleṣu
bījaṁ saṅkarṣaṇasya ca
haimāny aṇḍāni jātāni
mahā-bhūtāvṛtāni tu

tat—of Him (Mahā-Viṣṇu); *roma-bila-jāleṣu*—in the pores of the skin; *bījam*—the seeds; *saṅkarṣaṇasya*—of Saṅkarṣaṇa; *ca*—and; *haimāni*—golden; *aṇḍāni*—eggs or sperms; *jātāni*—born; *mahā-bhūta*—by the five great elements; *āvṛtāni*—covered; *tu*—certainly.

The spiritual seeds of Saṅkarṣaṇa existing in the pores of skin of Mahā-Viṣṇu, are born as so many golden sperms. These sperms are covered with five great elements.

PURPORT

The prime divine *avatāra* lying in the spiritual Causal Ocean is such a great affair that in the pores of His divine form spring up myriads of seeds of the universes. Those series of universes are the perverted reflections of the infinite transcendental region. As long as they remain embedded in His divine form they embody the principle of spiritual reflection having the form of golden eggs. Nevertheless by the creative desire of Mahā-Viṣṇu the minute particles of the great elements, which are constituents of the mundane efficient and material causal principles, envelop them. When those golden sperms, coming out with the exhalation of Mahā-Viṣṇu, enter into the unlimited accommodating chamber of the limited potency (Māyā) they become enlarged by the nonconglomerate great elements.

TEXT 14

प्रत्यण्डमेवमेकांशादेकांशाद्विशति स्वयम् ।
सहस्रमूर्धा विश्वात्मा महाविष्णुः सनातनः ॥१४॥

praty-aṇḍam evam ekāṁśād
ekāṁśād viśati svayam
sahasra-mūrdhā viśvātmā
mahā-viṣṇuḥ sanātanaḥ

prati—each; *aṇḍam*—egglike universe; *evam*—thus; *eka-aṁśāt eka-aṁśāt*—as His own separate subjective portions; *viśati*—enters; *svayam*—personally; *sahasra-mūrdhā*—possessing thousands of heads; *viśva-ātmā*—the Supersoul of the universe; *mahā-viṣṇuḥ*—Mahā-Viṣṇu; *sanātanaḥ*—eternal.

The same Mahā-Viṣṇu entered into each universe as His own separate subjective portions. The divine portions, that entered

into each universe are possessed of His majestic extension, i.e., they are the eternal universal soul Mahā-Viṣṇu, possessing thousands of thousands of heads.

PURPORT

Mahā-Viṣṇu lying in the spiritual Causal Ocean is the subjective portion of Mahā-Saṅkarṣaṇa. He entered, as His own subjective portions, into those universes. These individual portions all represent the second divine *puruṣa* lying in the ocean of conception and is identical with Mahā-Viṣṇu in every respect. He is also spoken of as the divine guide, from within, of all souls.

TEXT 15

वामाङ्गादसृजद्विष्णुं दक्षिणाङ्गात्प्रजापतिम् ।
ज्योतिर्लिङ्गमयं शम्भुं कूर्चदेशादवासृजत् ॥१५॥

vāmāṅgād asṛjad viṣṇuṁ
dakṣiṇāṅgāt prajāpatim
jyotir-liṅga-mayaṁ śambhuṁ
kūrca-deśād avāsṛjat

vāma-aṅgāt—from His left limb; *asṛjat*—He created; *viṣṇum*—Lord Viṣṇu; *dakṣiṇa-aṅgāt*—from His right limb; *prajāpatim*—Hiraṇyagarbha Brahmā; *jyotiḥ-liṅga*—the divine masculine manifested halo; *mayam*—comprising; *śambhum*—Śambhu; *kūrca-deśāt*—from the space between His two eyebrows; *avā-sṛjat*—He created.

The same Mahā-Viṣṇu created Viṣṇu from His left limb, Brahmā, the first progenitor of beings, from His right limb and, from the space between His two eyebrows, Śambhu, the divine masculine manifested halo.

PURPORT

The divine *puruṣa*, lying in the ocean of milk, the same who is the regulator of all individual souls, is Śrī Viṣṇu; and Hiraṇyagarbha, the seminal principle, the portion of the Supreme Lord, is the prime progenitor who is different from the four-faced Brahmā. This same Hiraṇyagarbha is the principle of seminal creating energy of every Brahmā belonging to each of the infinity of universes. The divine masculine manifested halo, Śambhu, is the plenary manifestation of his prototype Śambhu, the same as the primary divine masculine generative symbol Śambhu whose nature has already been described. Viṣṇu is the integral subjective portion of Mahā-Viṣṇu. Hence He is the great Lord of all the other lords. The progenitor (Brahmā) and Śambhu are the dislocated portions of Mahā-Viṣṇu. Hence they are gods with delegated functions. His own potency being on the left side of Godhead, Viṣṇu appears in the left limb of Mahā-Viṣṇu from the unalloyed essence of His spiritual (*cit*) potency. Viṣṇu, who is Godhead Himself, is the inner guiding oversoul of every individual soul. He is the Personality of Godhead described in the *Vedas* as being of the measure of a thumb. He is the nourisher. The *karmīs* (elevationists) worship Him as Nārāyaṇa, the Lord of sacrifices, and the *yogīs* desire to merge their identities in Him as Paramātmā, by the process of their meditative trance.

TEXT 16

अहङ्कारात्मकं विश्वं तस्मादेतद्व्यजायत ॥१६॥

ahaṅkārātmakaṁ viśvaṁ
tasmād etad vyajāyata

ahaṅkāra—the mundane egotistic principle; *ātmakam*—enshrining; *viśvam*—universe; *tasmāt*—from that (Śambhu); *etat*—this; *vyajāyata*—has originated.

The function of Śambhu in relation to jīvas is that this universe enshrining the mundane egotistic principle has originated from Śambhu.

PURPORT

The basic principle is the Supreme Lord Himself who is the embodiment of the principle of existence of all entities devoid of separating egotisms. In this mundane world the appearance of individual entities as separated egotistic symbols, is the limited perverted reflection of the unalloyed spiritual (*cit*) potency; and, as representing the primal masculine divine generative function Śambhu, it is united to the accommodating principle, viz., the mundane female organ which is the perverted reflection of the spiritual (*cit*) potency, Ramādevī. At this function Śambhu is nothing but the mere material causal principle embodying the extension in the shape of ingredient as matter. Again when in course of the progressive evolution of mundane creation each universe is manifested, then in the principle of Śambhu, born of the space between the two eyebrows of Viṣṇu, there appears the manifestation of the personality of Rudra; yet under all circumstances Śambhu fully enshrines the mundane egotistic principle. The innumerable *jīvas* as spiritual particles emanating from the oversoul in the form of pencils of rays of effulgence, have no relation with the mundane world when they come to know themselves to be the eternal servants of the Supreme Lord. They are then incorporated into the realm of Vaikuṇṭha. But when they desire to lord it over Māyā, forgetting their real identity, the egotistic principle Śambhu entering into their entities makes them identify themselves as separated enjoyers of mundane entities. Hence Śambhu is the primary principle of the egotistic mundane universe and of perverted egotism in *jīvas* that identifies itself with their limited material bodies.

TEXT 17

अथ तैस्त्रिविधैर्वेशैर्लीलामुद्वहतः किल ।
योगनिद्रा भगवती तस्य श्रीरिव सङ्गता ॥१७॥

atha tais tri-vidhair veśair
līlām udvahataḥ kila
yoga-nidrā bhagavatī
tasya śrīr iva saṅgatā

atha—thereupon; *taiḥ*—with those; *tri-vidhaiḥ*—threefold; *veśaiḥ*—forms; *līlām*—pastimes; *udvahataḥ*—carrying on; *kila*—indeed; *yoga-nidrā*—Yoganidrā; *bhagavatī*—full of the ecstatic trance of eternal bliss; *tasya*—of Him; *śrīḥ*—the goddess of fortune; *iva*—like; *saṅgatā*—consorted with.

Thereupon the same great personal Godhead, assuming the threefold forms of Viṣṇu, Prajāpati and Śambhu, entering into the mundane universe, plays the pastimes of preservation, creation and destruction of this world. This pastime is contained in the mundane world. Hence, it being perverted, the Supreme Lord, identical with Mahā-Viṣṇu, prefers to consort with the goddess Yoganidrā, the constituent of His own spiritual [cit] potency full of the ecstatic trance of eternal bliss appertaining to His own divine personality.

PURPORT

The dislocated portions of the Divinity, viz., Prajāpati and Śambhu, both identifying themselves as entities who are separate from the divine essence, sport with their respective nonspiritual (*acit*) consorts, viz., Sāvitrī-devī and Umā-devī, the perverted reflections of the spiritual (*cit*) potency. The Supreme Lord Viṣṇu is the only Lord of the spiritual (*cit*) potency, Ramā or Lakṣmī.

TEXT 18

सिसृक्षायां ततो नाभेस्तस्य पद्मं विनिर्ययौ ।
तन्नालं हेमनलिनं ब्रह्मणो लोकमद्भुतम् ॥१८॥

sisṛkṣāyāṁ tato nābhes
tasya padmaṁ viniryayau
tan-nālaṁ hema-nalinaṁ
brahmaṇo lokam adbhutam

sisṛkṣāyām—when there was the will to create; *tataḥ*—then; *nābheḥ*—from the navel; *tasya*—of Him; *padmam*—a lotus; *viniryayau*—came out; *tat-nālam*—its stem; *hema-nalinam*—like a golden lotus; *brahmaṇaḥ*—of Brahmā; *lokam*—the abode; *adbhutam*—wonderful.

When Viṣṇu lying in the ocean of milk wills to create this universe, a golden lotus springs from His navel-pit. The golden lotus with its stem is the abode of Brahmā representing Brahmaloka or Satyaloka.

"Gold" here means the dim reflection of pure cognition.

TEXT 19

तत्त्वानि पूर्वरूढानि कारणानि परस्परम् ।
समवायाप्रयोगाच्च विभिन्नानि पृथक् पृथक् ॥
चिच्छक्त्या सज्जमानोऽथ भगवान् आदिपूरुषः ।
योजयन् मायया देवो योगनिद्रामकल्पयत् ॥१९॥

tattvāni pūrva-rūḍhāni
kāraṇāni parasparam
samavāyāprayogāc ca
vibhinnāni pṛthak pṛthak

cic-chaktyā sajjamāno 'tha
bhagavān ādi-pūruṣaḥ
yojayan māyayā devo
yoga-nidrām akalpayat

tattvāni—elements; *pūrva-rūḍhāni*—previously created; *kāraṇāni*—causes; *parasparam*—mutually; *samavāya*—of the process of conglomeration; *aprayogāt*—from the nonapplication; *ca*—and; *vibhinnāni*—separate; *pṛthak pṛthak*—one from another; *cit-śaktyā*—with His spiritual potency; *sajjamānaḥ*—associating; *atha*—then; *bhagavān*—the Supreme Personality of Godhead; *ādi-pūruṣaḥ*—the primal Godhead; *yojayan*—causing to join; *māyayā*—with Māyā; *devaḥ*—the Lord; *yoga-nidrām*—Yoganidrā; *akalpayat*—He consorted with.

Before their conglomeration the primary elements in their nascent state remained originally separate entities. Nonapplication of the conglomerating process is the cause of their separate existence. Divine Mahā-Viṣṇu, primal Godhead, through association with His own spiritual [cit] potency, moved Māyā and by the application of the conglomerating principle created those different entities in their state of cooperation. And after that He Himself consorted with Yoganidrā by way of His eternal dalliance with His spiritual [cit] potency.

PURPORT

Mayādhyakṣeṇa prakṛtiḥ sūyate sa-carācaram: "The mundane energy *prakṛti* gives birth to this universe of animate and inanimate beings by My direction." The purport of this *śloka* of the

Gītā is that Māyā, the perverted reflection of spiritual (*cit*) potency, was at first inactive and her extension of matter constituting the material cause was also in the separately dislocated state. In accordance with the will of Kṛṣṇa this world is manifested as the resultant of the union of the efficient and the material causal principles of Māyā. In spite of that, the Supreme Lord Himself remains united with His *cit* potency, Yoganidrā. The word *yoganidrā* or *yogamāyā* indicates as follows: The nature of *cit* potency is manifestive of the Absolute Truth, while the nature of her perverted reflection, Māyā, is envelopment in the gloom of ignorance. When Kṛṣṇa desires to manifest something in the mundane ignorance-wrapt affairs, He does this by the conjunction of His spiritual potency with His inactive nonspiritual potency. This is known as Yogamāyā. It carries a twofold notion, namely, transcendental notion and mundane inert notion. Kṛṣṇa Himself, His subjective portions and those *jīvas* who are His unalloyed separated particles, realize the transcendental notion in that conjunction, while conditioned souls feel the mundane inert notion. The external coating of transcendental knowledge in the conscious activities of conditioned souls, bears the name of Yoganidrā. This is also an influence of the *cit* potency of the Divinity. This principle will be more elaborately considered hereafter.

TEXT 20

योजयित्वा तु तान्येव प्रविवेश स्वयं गुहाम् ।
गुहां प्रविष्टे तस्मिंस्तु जीवात्मा प्रतिबुध्यते ॥२०॥

yojayitvā tu tāny eva
praviveśa svayaṁ guhām
guhāṁ praviṣṭe tasmiṁs tu
jīvātmā pratibudhyate

yojayitvā—after conglomerating; *tu*—then; *tāni*—them; *eva*—certainly; *praviveśa*—He entered; *svayam*—Himself; *guhām*—the hidden cavity; *guhām*—the hidden cavity; *praviṣṭe*—after He entered; *tasmin*—within that; *tu*—then; *jīva-ātmā*—the *jīvas*; *pratibudhyate*—were awakened.

By conglomerating all those separate entities He manifested the innumerable mundane universes and Himself entered into the inmost recess of every extended conglomerate [viraḍ-vigraha]. At that time those jīvas who had lain dormant during the cataclysm were awakened.

PURPORT

The word *guhā* (hidden cavity) bears various interpretations in the *śāstras*. In some portions the nonmanifestive pastimes of the Lord is called *guhā* and elsewhere the resting place of the indwelling spirit of all individual souls, is named *guhā*. In many places the inmost recesses of the heart of each individual is termed *guhā*. The main point is that the place which is hidden from the view of men in general, is designated *guhā*. Those *jīvas* that were merged in Hari at the end of the life of Brahmā in the great cataclysm during the preceding great age of the universe, reappeared in this world in accordance with their former fruitive desires.

TEXT 21

स नित्यो नित्यसम्बन्धः प्रकृतिश्च परैव सा ॥२१॥

sa nityo nitya-sambandhaḥ
prakṛtiś ca paraiva sā

saḥ—that (*jīva*); *nityaḥ*—eternal; *nitya-sambandhaḥ*—possessing an eternal relationship; *prakṛtiḥ*—potency; *ca*—and;

parā—spiritual; *eva*—certainly; *sā*—that.

The same jīva is eternal and is for eternity and without a beginning joined to the Supreme Lord by the tie of an eternal kinship. He is transcendental spiritual potency.

PURPORT

Just as the sun is eternally associated with his rays so the transcendental Supreme Lord is eternally joined with the *jīvas*. The *jīvas* are the infinitesimal particles of His spiritual effulgence and are, therefore, not perishable like mundane things. *Jīvas*, being particles of Godhead's effulgent rays, exhibit on a minute scale the qualities of the Divinity. Hence *jīvas* are identical with the principles of knowledge, knower, egoism, enjoyer, meditator and doer. Kṛṣṇa is the all-pervading, all-extending Supreme Lord; while *jīvas* have a different nature from His, being His atomic particles. That eternal relationship consists in this that the Supreme Lord is the eternal master and *jīvas* are His eternal servants. *Jīvas* have also sufficient eligibility in respect of the mellow quality of the Divinity. *Apareyam itas tv anyāṁ prakṛtiṁ viddhi me parām*. By this verse of the *Gītā* it is made known that *jīvas* are His transcendental potency. All the qualities of the unalloyed soul are above the eightfold qualities such as egotism, etc., pertaining to His *acit* potency. Hence the *jīva* potency, though very small in magnitude, is still superior to *acit* potency or Māyā. This potency has another name, viz., *taṭasthā* or marginal potency, being located on the line demarcating the spheres of the spiritual and mundane potencies. He is susceptible to the influence of the material energy owing to his small magnitude. But so long as he remains submissive to Kṛṣṇa, the Lord of Māyā, he is not liable to the influence of Māyā. The worldly afflictions, births and rebirths are the concomitants of the fettered condition of souls fallen into the clutches of the deluding potency from a time that has no beginning.

TEXT 22

एवं सर्वात्मसम्बन्धं नाभ्यां पद्मं हरेरभूत् ।
तत्र ब्रह्माभवद्भूयश्चतुर्वेदी चतुर्मुखः ॥२२॥

evaṁ sarvātma-sambandhaṁ
nābhyāṁ padmaṁ harer abhūt
tatra brahmābhavad bhūyaś
catur-vedī catur-mukhaḥ

evam—thus; *sarva-ātma*—with all souls; *sambandham*—related; *nābhyām*—from the navel; *padmam*—a lotus; *hareḥ*—of Viṣṇu; *abhūt*—sprung up; *tatra*—there; *brahmā*—Brahmā; *abhavat*—was born; *bhūyaḥ*—again; *catuḥ-vedī*—versed in the four *Vedas*; *catuḥ-mukhaḥ*—four-faced.

The divine lotus which springs from the navel-pit of Viṣṇu is in every way related by the spiritual tie with all souls and is the origin of four-faced Brahmā versed in the four Vedas.

PURPORT

The same divine lotus originating from the divine person entered into the hidden recess, is the superior plane of aggregation of all individual souls. The four-faced Brahmā, the image of self-enjoyment, derives his origin from the prototype Brahmā or Hiraṇyagarbha, the mundane seminal principle, who regards the aggregate of all mundane entities as his own proper body. The delegated godship of Brahmā as well as his being the dislocated portion of Kṛṣṇa, are also established.

TEXT 23

सञ्जातो भगवच्छक्त्या तत्कालं किल चोदितः ।
सिसृक्षायां मतिं चक्रे पूर्वसंस्कारसंस्कृतः ।

दद‍र्श केवलं ध्वान्तं नान्यत्किमपि सर्वतः ॥२३॥

sañjāto bhagavac-chaktyā
tat-kālaṁ kila coditaḥ
sisṛkṣāyāṁ matiṁ cakre
pūrva-saṁskāra-saṁskṛtaḥ
dadarśa kevalaṁ dhvāntaṁ
nānyat kim api sarvataḥ

sañjātaḥ—on being born; *bhagavat-śaktyā*—by the divine potency; *tat-kālam*—at that time; *kila*—indeed; *coditaḥ*—being guided; *sisṛkṣāyām*—to the act of creation; *matim*—his mind; *cakre*—turned; *pūrva-saṁskāra-saṁskṛtaḥ*—under the impulse of previous impressions; *dadarśa*—he saw; *kevalam*—only; *dhvāntam*—darkness; *na*—not; *anyat*—else; *kim api*—anything; *sarvataḥ*—in every direction.

On coming out of the lotus, Brahmā, being guided by the divine potency tuned his mind to the act of creation under the impulse of previous impressions. But he could see nothing but darkness in every direction.

PURPORT

Bra̧hmā's impulse for creation arises solely from his previous impressions. All *jīvas* get their nature conformably to their impressions of previous births and accordingly their activity can have a beginning. It is called "the unseen" or the result of one's previous deeds. His natural impulse is formed according to the nature of the deeds done by him in the previous *kalpa*. Some of the eligible *jīvas* also attain to the office of Brahmā in this way.

TEXT 24

उवाच पुरतस्तस्मै तस्य दिव्या सरस्वती ।

कामकृष्णाय गोविन्द हे गोपीजन इत्यपि ।
वल्लभाय प्रिया वह्नेर्मन्त्रं ते दास्यति प्रियम् ॥२४॥

uvāca puratas tasmai
tasya divyā sarasvatī
kāma-kṛṣṇāya govinda
he gopī-jana ity api
vallabhāya priyā vahner
mantraṁ te dāsyati priyam

uvāca—said; *purataḥ*—in front; *tasmai*—to him; *tasya*—of Him (the Supreme Lord); *divyā*—divine; *sarasvatī*—the goddess of learning; *kāma*—the *kāma-bīja* (*klīṁ*); *kṛṣṇāya*—to Kṛṣṇa; *govinda-govindāya*, to Govinda; *he*—O; *gopī-jana*—of the *gopīs; iti*—thus; *api*—also; *vallabhāya*—to the dear one; *priyā vahneḥ*—the wife of Agni, Svāhā (the word *svāhā* is uttered while offering oblations); *mantram*—*mantra; te*—to you; *dāsyati*—will give; *priyam*—the heart's desire.

Then the goddess of learning Sarasvatī, the divine consort of the Supreme Lord, said thus to Brahmā who saw nothing but gloom in all directions, "O Brahmā, this mantra, viz., klīṁ kṛṣṇāya govindāya gopī-jana-vallabhāya svāhā, will assuredly fulfill your heart's desire."

PURPORT

The *mantra*, consisting of the eighteen divine letters prefixed by the *kāma-bīja*, is alone superexcellent. It has a twofold aspect. One aspect is that it tends to make the pure soul run after all-attractive Śrī Kṛṣṇa, the Lord of Gokula and the divine milk-maids. This is the acme of the spiritual tendency of *jīvas*. When the devotee is free from all sorts of mundane desires and willing to serve the Lord he attains the fruition of his heart's desire, viz., the love of Kṛṣṇa. But in the case of the devotee who is

veṇum—the flute; *vādayantam*—playing; *mukha-ambuje*—at His lotus mouth; *vilāsinī-gaṇa*—by the *gopīs; vṛtam*—surrounded; *svaiḥ svaiḥ*—own respective; *aṁśaiḥ*—by subjective portions; *abhiṣṭutam*—worshiped.

Brahmā, being desirous of satisfying Govinda, practiced the cultural acts for Kṛṣṇa in Goloka, Lord of Śvetadvīpa, for a long time. His meditation ran thus, "There exists a divine lotus of a thousand petals, augmented by millions of filaments, in the transcendental land of Goloka. On its whorl, there exists a great divine throne on which is seated Śrī Kṛṣṇa, the form of eternal effulgence of transcendental bliss, playing on His divine flute resonant with the divine sound, with His lotus mouth. He is worshiped by His amorous milkmaids with their respective subjective portions and extensions and also by His external energy [who stays outside] embodying all mundane qualities."

PURPORT

Although the object of meditation is fully transcendental, yet owing to her nature which is permeated with the quality of active mundane hankering, Māyā, the nonspiritual potency of Kṛṣṇa, embodying the principles of mixed *sattva*, *rajas*, and *tamas*, in the forms of Durgā, and other nonspiritual powers, meditated on the Supreme Lord Kṛṣṇa as the object of their worship. So long as there is any trace of mundane desire in one's heart, it is the object of worship of Māyādevī (Durgā) who has to be worshiped by such a person; nevertheless the fulfillment of one's heart's desire results from the worship of the object of worship of Māyādevī, and not from the worship of Māyādevī herself. This is in accordance with the *śloka*, *akāmaḥ sarva-kāmo vā mokṣa-kāma udāra-dhīḥ / tīvreṇa bhakti-yogena yajeta puruṣaṁ param*. The meaning of this *śloka* of the *Bhāgavatam* is that though other gods, as distinct manifestations of the Supreme Lord, are bestowers of sundry specific boons, yet a sensible person should worship the all powerful Supreme Lord, giver of all good, with unalloyed devotion, without worshiping those mundane gift-giving deities. Accordingly, Brahmā meditated upon Kṛṣṇa in Goloka, the object of the worship, from a distance, of Māyādevī. True devotion is unalloyed devotional activity free from all mundane desire. The devotion of Brahmā, etc., is not unmixed devotion. But there is a stage of unmixed predilection even in devotion for the attainment of one's selfish desire. This has been fully described in the concluding five *ślokas* of this work. That is the easiest method of divine service, prior to the attainment of self-realization, by fallen souls.

TEXT 27

अथ वेणुनिनादस्य त्रयीमूर्तिमयी गतिः ।
स्फुरन्ती प्रविवेशाशु मुखाब्जानि स्वयम्भुवः ॥
गायत्रीं गायतस्तस्मादधिगत्य सरोजजः ।
संस्कृतश्चादिगुरुणा द्विजतामगमत्ततः ॥२७॥

atha veṇu-ninādasya
trayī-mūrti-mayī gatiḥ
sphurantī praviveśāśu
mukhābjāni svayambhuvaḥ

gāyatrīṁ gāyatas tasmād
adhigatya sarojajaḥ
saṁskṛtaś cādi-guruṇā
dvijatām agamat tataḥ

atha—then; *veṇu-ninādasya*—of the sound of the flute; *trayī-mūrti-mayī*—the mother of the three *Vedas; gatiḥ*—the means (the Gāyatrī *mantra*); *sphurantī*—being made manifest; *praviveśa*—entered; *āśu*—quickly; *mukha-abjāni*—the lotus faces; *svayambhuvaḥ*—of Brahmā; *gāyatrīm*—the Gāyatrī; *gāyataḥ*—sounding; *tasmāt*—from Him (Śrī Kṛṣṇa); *adhigatya*—having received; *saroja-jaḥ*—the lotus-born (Brahmā); *saṁskṛtaḥ*—initiated; *ca*—and; *ādi-guruṇā*—by the primal preceptor; *dvijatām*—the status of the twice-born; *agamat*—attained; *tataḥ*—thereafter.

Then Gāyatrī, mother of the Vedas, being made manifest, i.e. imparted, by the divine sound of the flute of Śrī Kṛṣṇa, entered into the lotus mouth of Brahmā, born from himself, through his eight ear-holes. The lotus-born Brahmā having received the Gāyatrī, sprung from the flute-song of Śrī Kṛṣṇa, attained the status of the twice-born, having been initiated by the supreme primal preceptor, Godhead Himself.

PURPORT

The sound of Kṛṣṇa's flute is the transcendental blissful sound; hence the archetype of all *Veda*, is present in it. The Gāyatrī is Vedic rhythm. It contains a brief meditation and prayer. *Kāma-gāyatrī* is the highest of all the Gāyatrīs, because the meditation and prayer contained in it are full of the perfect transcendental sportive activities which are not to be found in any other Gāyatrī. The Gāyatrī that is attained as the sequel of the eighteen-lettered *mantra* is *kāma-gāyatrī* which runs thus: *klīṁ kāma-devāya vidmahe puṣpa-bāṇāya dhīmahi tan no 'naṅgaḥ pracodayāt*. In this Gāyatrī, the realization of the transcendental pastimes of Śrī Gopījana-vallabha after perfect meditation and the prayer for the attainment of the transcendental god of love are indicated. In the spiritual world there is no better mode of endeavor for securing the superexcellent *rasa*-bedewed love. As soon as that Gāyatrī entered into the ear-holes of Brahmā, he became the twice-born and began to chant the Gāyatrī. Whoever has received the same Gāyatrī in reality, has attained his spiritual rebirth. The status of a twice-born that is obtained in accordance with one's worldly nature and lineage, by the fettered souls in this mundane world, is far inferior to that of the twice-born who obtains admission into the transcendental world; because the initiation or acquisition of transcendental birth as a result of spiritual initiation is the highest of glories in as much as the *jīva* is thereby enabled to attain to the transcendental realm.

TEXT 28

त्रय्या प्रबुद्धोऽथ विधिर्विज्ञाततत्त्वसागरः ।
तुष्टाव वेदसारेण स्तोत्रेणानेन केशवम् ॥२८॥

trayyā prabuddho 'tha vidhir
vijñāta-tattva-sāgaraḥ
tuṣṭāva veda-sāreṇa
stotreṇānena keśavam

trayyā—by the embodiment of the three *Vedas; prabuddhaḥ*—enlightened; *atha*—then; *vidhiḥ*—Brahmā; *vijñāta*—acquainted with; *tattva-sāgaraḥ*—the ocean of truth; *tuṣṭāva*—worshiped; *veda-sāreṇa*—which is the essence of all *Vedas; stotreṇa*—by the hymn; *anena*—this; *keśavam*—Śrī Kṛṣṇa.

Enlightened by the recollection of that Gāyatrī, embodying the three Vedas, Brahmā became acquainted with the expanse of the ocean of truth. Then he worshiped Śrī Kṛṣṇa, the essence of all Vedas, with this hymn.

PURPORT

Brahmā thought thus within himself, "By the recollection of *kāma-gāyatrī* it seems to me that I am the eternal maidservant of Kṛṣṇa." Though the other mysteries in regard to the condition of the maidservant of Kṛṣṇa were not revealed to him, Brahmā, by dint of his searching self-consciousness, became well acquainted with the ocean of truth. All the truths of the *Vedas* were revealed to him and with the help of those essences of the *Vedas* he offered this hymn to the Supreme Lord Śrī Kṛṣṇa. Śrīmān Mahāprabhu has taught this hymn to His favorite disciples in as much as it fully contains all the transcendental truths regarding the Vaiṣṇava philosophy. Readers are requested to study and try to enter into the spirit of his hymn with great care and attention, as a regular daily function.

TEXT 29

चिन्तामणिप्रकरसद्मसु कल्पवृक्ष-
लक्षावृतेषु सुरभीरभिपालयन्तम् ।
लक्ष्मीसहस्रशतसम्भ्रमसेव्यमानं
गोविन्दमादिपुरुषं तमहं भजामि ॥२९॥

cintāmaṇi-prakara-sadmasu kalpa-vṛkṣa-
lakṣāvṛteṣu surabhīr abhipālayantam
lakṣmī-sahasra-śata-sambhrama-sevyamānaṁ
govindam ādi-puruṣaṁ tam ahaṁ bhajāmi

cintāmaṇi—touchstone; *prakara*—groups made of; *sadmasu*—in abodes; *kalpa-vṛkṣa*—of desire trees; *lakṣa*—by millions; *āvṛteṣu*—surrounded; *surabhīḥ*—surabhi cows; *abhipālayantam*—tending; *lakṣmī*—of goddesses of fortune; *sahasra*—of thousands; *śata*—by hundreds; *sambhrama*—with great respect; *sevyamānam*—being served; *govindam*—Govinda; *ādi-puruṣam*—the original person; *tam*—Him; *aham*—I; *bhajāmi*—worship.

I worship Govinda, the primeval Lord, the first progenitor who is tending the cows, yielding all desire, in abodes built with spiritual gems, surrounded by millions of purpose trees, always

served with great reverence and affection by hundreds of thousands of lakṣmīs or gopīs.

PURPORT

By the word *cintāmaṇi* is meant "transcendental gem." Just as Māyā builds this mundane universe with the five material elements, so the spiritual (*cit*) potency has built the spiritual world of transcendental gems. The *cintāmaṇi* which serves as material in the building of the abode of the Supreme Lord of Goloka, is a far rarer and more agreeable entity than the philosopher's stone. The purpose tree yields only the fruits of piety, wealth, fulfillment of desire and liberation; but the purpose trees in the abode of Kṛṣṇa bestow innumerable fruits in the shape of checkered divine love. *Kāma-dhenus* (cows yielding the fulfillment of desire) give milk when they are milked; but the *kāma-dhenus* of Goloka pour forth oceans of milk in the shape of the fountain of love showering transcendental bliss that does away with the hunger and thirst of all pure devotees. The words *lakṣa* and *sahasra-śata* signify endless numbers. The word *sambhrama* or *sādara* indicates "being saturated with love." Here *lakṣmī* denotes *gopī*. *Ādi-puruṣa* means, "He who is the primeval Lord."

TEXT 30

वेणुं क्वणन्तमरविन्ददलायताक्षं
बर्हावतंसमसिताम्बुदसुन्दराङ्गम् ।
कन्दर्पकोटिकमनीयविशेषशोभं
गोविन्दमादिपुरुषं तमहं भजामि ॥३०॥

veṇuṁ kvaṇantam aravinda-dalāyatākṣaṁ
barhāvataṁsam asitāmbuda-sundarāṅgam
kandarpa-koṭi-kamanīya-viśeṣa-śobhaṁ
govindam ādi-puruṣaṁ tam ahaṁ bhajāmi

veṇum—the flute; *kvaṇantam*—playing; *aravinda-dala*—(like) lotus petals; *āyata*—blooming; *akṣam*—whose eyes; *barha*—a peacock's feather; *avataṁsam*—whose ornament on the head; *asita-ambuda*—(tinged with the hue of) blue clouds; *sundara*—beautiful; *aṅgam*—whose figure; *kandarpa*—of Cupids; *koṭi*—millions; *kamanīya*—charming; *viśeṣa*—unique; *śobham*—whose loveliness; *govindam*—Govinda; *ādi-puruṣam*—the original person; *tam*—Him; *aham*—I; *bhajāmi*—worship.

I worship Govinda, the primeval Lord, who is adept in playing on His flute, with blooming eyes like lotus petals with head decked with peacock's feather, with the figure of beauty tinged with the hue of blue clouds, and His unique loveliness charming millions of Cupids.

PURPORT

The matchless beauty of Kṛṣṇa, the Supreme Lord of Goloka, is being described. Kṛṣṇa, the all-pervading cognition, has a spiritual form of His own. The form of Kṛṣṇa is not a fanciful creation of imagination formed after visualizing the beautiful things of the world. What Brahmā saw in his ecstatic trance of pure devotion, is being described. Kṛṣṇa is engaged in playing upon His flute. That flute by his enchanting musical sound attracts the hearts of all living beings. Just as a lotus petal produces a pleasant sight, so the two beautiful eyes of Kṛṣṇa who causes the manifestation of our spiritual vision, display the unlimited splendor and beauty of His moonlike face. The loveliness that adorns His head with peacock feather figures, the corresponding feature of the spiritual beauty of Kṛṣṇa. Just as a mass of blue clouds offers a specifically soothing, pleasant view, the complexion of Kṛṣṇa is analogously tinged with a spiritual dark-blue color. The beauty and loveliness of Kṛṣṇa is far more enchanting that that of Cupid multiplied a millionfold.

TEXT 31

आलोलचन्द्रकलसद्वनमाल्यवंशी-
रत्नाङ्गदं प्रणयकेलिकलाविलासम् ।
श्यामं त्रिभङ्गललितं नियतप्रकाशं
गोविन्दमादिपुरुषं तमहं भजामि ॥३१॥

ālola-candraka-lasad-vanamālya-vaṁśī-
ratnāṅgadaṁ praṇaya-keli-kalā-vilāsam
śyāmaṁ tri-bhaṅga-lalitaṁ niyata-prakāśaṁ
govindam ādi-puruṣaṁ tam ahaṁ bhajāmi

ālola—swinging; *candraka*—with a moon-locket; *lasat*—beautified; *vana-mālya*—a garland of flowers; *vaṁśī*—flute; *ratna-aṅgadam*—adorned with jeweled ornaments; *praṇaya*—of love; *keli-kalā*—in pastimes; *vilāsam*—who always revels; *śyāmam*—Śyāmasundara; *tri-bhaṅga*—bending in three places; *lalitam*—graceful; *niyata*—eternally; *prakāśam*—manifest; *govindam*—Govinda; *ādi-puruṣam*—the original person; *tam*—Him; *aham*—I; *bhajāmi*—worship.

I worship Govinda, the primeval Lord, round whose neck is swinging a garland of flowers beautified with the moon-locket, whose two hands are adorned with the flute and jeweled ornaments, who always revels in pastimes of love, whose graceful threefold-bending form of Śyāmasundara is eternally manifest.

In the *śloka* beginning with *cintāmaṇi-prakara* the transcendental region and the spiritual names of Govinda, in the *śloka* beginning with *veṇuṁ kvaṇantam*, the eternal beautiful form of Govinda and in this *śloka* the amorous pastimes of Govinda, the embodiment of His sixty-four excellences, have been described. All the spiritual affairs that come within the scope of description in the narration of the ecstatic mellow quality (*rasa*) are included in the spiritual amorous sports of Govinda.

TEXT 32

अङ्गानि यस्य सकलेन्द्रियवृत्तिमन्ति
पश्यन्ति पान्ति कलयन्ति चिरं जगन्ति ।
आनन्दचिन्मयसदुज्ज्वलविग्रहस्य
गोविन्दमादिपुरुषं तमहं भजामि ॥३२॥

aṅgāni yasya sakalendriya-vṛtti-manti
paśyanti pānti kalayanti ciraṁ jaganti
ānanda-cinmaya-sad-ujjvala-vigrahasya
govindam ādi-puruṣaṁ tam ahaṁ bhajāmi

aṅgāni—the limbs; *yasya*—of whom; *sakala-indriya*—of all the organs; *vṛtti-manti*—possessing the functions; *paśyanti*—see; *pānti*—maintain; *kalayanti*—manifest; *ciram*—eternally; *jaganti*—the universes; *ānanda*—bliss; *cit*—truth; *maya*—full of; *sat*—substantiality; *ujjvala*—full of dazzling splendor; *vigrahasya*—whose form; *govindam*—Govinda; *ādi-puruṣam*—the original person; *tam*—Him; *aham*—I; *bhajāmi*—worship.

I worship Govinda, the primeval Lord, whose transcendental form is full of bliss, truth, substantiality and is thus full of the most dazzling splendor. Each of the limbs of that transcendental figure possesses in Himself, the full-fledged functions of all the organs, and eternally sees, maintains and manifests the infinite universes, both spiritual and mundane.

PURPORT

For want of a taste of things spiritual, a grave doubt arises in the minds of those who are enchained by worldly knowledge.

On hearing a narration of the pastimes of Kṛṣṇa they think that the truth (*tattva*) regarding Kṛṣṇa is the mental concoction of certain learned scholars, created by their imaginative brains out of material drawn from the mundane principles. With the object of removing this harmful doubt, Brahmā in this and the three following *ślokas*, after distinguishing between the two things, viz., spirit and matter, in a rational manner, has tried to make one understand the pure *līlā* of Kṛṣṇa, obtained by his unmixed ecstatic trance. Brahmā wants to say that the form of Kṛṣṇa is all existence, all-knowledge and all-bliss, whereas all mundane experiences are full of palpable ignorance. Although there is specific difference between the two, the fundamental truth is that spiritual affairs constitute the absolute source. Specification and variegatedness are ever present in it. By them are established the transcendental abode, form, name, quality and sports of Kṛṣṇa. It is only by a person, possessed of pure spiritual knowledge and freedom from any relationship with Māyā, that those amorous pastimes of Kṛṣṇa can at all be appreciated. The spiritual abode, the seat of pastimes, emanated from the *cit* potency and formed of *cintāmaṇi* (transcendental philosopher's stone), and the figure of Kṛṣṇa, are all spiritual. Just as Māyā is the perverted reflection of the spiritual potency, the variegatedness created by Māyā (ignorance) is also a perverted reflection of spiritual variegatedness. So a mere semblance of the spiritual variegatedness is only noticed in this mundane world. Notwithstanding such semblance the two are wholly different from one another. The unwholesomeness of matter is its defect; but in the spirit there is variegatedness which is free from any fault or contamination. The soul and the body of Kṛṣṇa are identical, whereas the body and soul of fallen creatures are not so. In the spiritual sphere there is no such difference as that between the body and soul, between the limbs and their proprietor, between the attributes and the object possessing them, of this world. But such difference really exists in the case of conditioned souls. Limbed though Kṛṣṇa is, His every limb is the whole entity. He performs all varieties of divine spiritual functions with every one of His limbs. Hence He is an indivisible whole and a perfect transcendental entity. Both *jīva*-soul and Kṛṣṇa are transcendental. So they belong to the same category. But they differ in this that the transcendental attributes exist in the *jīva*-soul in infinitesimally small degrees, whereas in Kṛṣṇa they are found in their fullest perfection. Those attributes manifest themselves in their proper infinitesimality only when the *jīva*-soul attains his unadulterated spiritual status. The *jīva*-soul attains the nearest approach to the absolute identity only when the spiritual force of ecstatic energy appears in him by the grace of Kṛṣṇa. Still Kṛṣṇa remains the object of universal homage by reason of His possession of certain unique attributes. These fourfold unrivaled attributes do not manifest themselves in Nārāyaṇa, the Lord of Vaikuṇṭha or in primeval *puruṣa-avatāras*, or in the highest deities such as Śiva, not to speak of *jīvas*.

TEXT 33

अद्वैतमच्युतमनादिमनन्तरूपम्
आद्यं पुराणपुरुषं नवयौवनं च ।
वेदेषु दुर्लभमदुर्लभमात्मभक्तौ
गोविन्दमादिपुरुषं तमहं भजामि ॥३३॥

advaitam acyutam anādim ananta-rūpam
ādyaṁ purāṇa-puruṣaṁ nava-yauvanaṁ ca
vedeṣu durlabham adurlabham ātma-bhaktau
govindam ādi-puruṣaṁ tam ahaṁ bhajāmi

advaitam—without a second; *acyutam*—without decay; *anādim*—without a beginning; *ananta-rūpam*—whose form is endless, or who possesses unlimited forms; *ādyam*—the beginning; *purāṇa-puruṣam*—the most ancient person; *nava-yauvanam*—a blooming youth; *ca*—also; *vedeṣu*—through the

Vedas; durlabham—inaccessible; *adurlabham*—not difficult to obtain; *ātma-bhaktau*—through pure devotion of the soul; *govindam*—Govinda; *ādi-puruṣam*—the original person; *tam*—Him; *aham*—I; *bhajāmi*—worship.

I worship Govinda, the primeval Lord, who is inaccessible to the Vedas, but obtainable by pure unalloyed devotion of the soul, who is without a second, who is not subject to decay, is without a beginning, whose form is endless, who is the beginning, and the eternal puruṣa; yet He is a person possessing the beauty of blooming youth.

PURPORT

Advaita means "indivisible truth who is knowledge absolute." Brahman, the infinite, emanates from Him as His effulgence and God-immanent (Paramātmā) as His constituent; but nevertheless He remains one and indivisible. *Acyuta* means that though myriads of *avatāras* emanate from Him as subjective portions and millions of *jīvas* as separated spiritual particles, still He remains intact as the undivided whole of fullest perfection. Though He indulges in exhibiting the pastimes of births, etc., still He is without a beginning. Though He disappears after the pastimes of His appearance, still He is eternal. Though without origin, yet He is with an origin in His pastime of appearance; and although eternal in essence, He is still a person in the full bloom of youth. The sum and substance of it is that though He possesses diverse and apparently mutually contradictory qualities, still they are in universal harmonious concordance by dint of His unthinkable potency. This is what is meant by *cid-dharma* (transcendental nature) as distinguished from the material. His graceful threefold-bending form with flute in hand, possesses eternal blooming youth and is above all unwholesomeness that is to be found in limited time and space. In the transcendental realm there is no past and future but only the unalloyed and immutable present time. In the transcendental sphere there is no distinction between the object and its qualities and no such identity as is found in the limited mundane region. Hence those qualities that seem to be apparently contradictory in the light of mundane conception limited by time and space, exist in agreeable and dainty concordance in the spiritual realm. How can the *jīva* realize such unprecedented existence? The limited intellectual function of the *jīva* is always contaminated by the influence of time and space and is, therefore, not in a position to shake off this limitedness. If the potency of cognitive function does not extend to the realization of the transcendental, what else can? In reply. Brahmā says that the transcendental Absolute is beyond the reach of the *Vedas*. The *Vedas* originate in sound and sound originates in the mundane ether. So the *Vedas* cannot present before us a direct view of the transcendental world (Goloka). It is only when the *Vedas* are imbued with the *cit* potency that they are enabled to deal with the transcendental. But Goloka reveals itself to every *jīva*-soul when he is under the influence of the spiritual cognitive potency joined to the essence of ecstatic energy. The ecstatic function of devotion is boundless and is surcharged with unalloyed transcendental knowledge. That knowledge reveals *goloka-tattva* (the principle of the highest transcendental) in unison with devotion, without asserting itself separately but as a subsidiary to unalloyed devotion.

TEXT 34

पन्थास्तु कोटिशतवत्सरसम्प्रगम्यो
वायोरथापि मनसो मुनिपुङ्गवानाम् ।
सोऽप्यस्ति यत्प्रपदसीम्न्यविचिन्त्यतत्त्वे
गोविन्दमादिपुरुषं तमहं भजामि ॥३४॥

panthās tu koṭi-śata-vatsara-sampragamyo
vāyor athāpi manaso muni-puṅgavānām

so 'py asti yat-prapada-sīmny avicintya-tattve
govindam ādi-puruṣaṁ tam ahaṁ bhajāmi

panthāḥ—the path; *tu*—but; *koṭi-śata*—thousands of millions; *vatsara*—of years; *sampragamyaḥ*—extending over; *vāyoḥ*—of wind; *atha api*—or; *manasaḥ*—of the mind; *muni-puṅgavānām*—of the foremost *jñānīs; saḥ*—that (path); *api*—only; *asti*—is; *yat*—of whom; *prapada*—of the toe; *sīmni*—to the tip; *avicintya-tattve*—beyond material conception; *govindam*—Govinda; *ādi-puruṣam*—the original person; *tam*—Him; *aham*—I; *bhajāmi*—worship.

I worship Govinda, the primeval Lord, only the tip of the toe of whose lotus feet is approached by the yogīs who aspire after the transcendental and betake themselves to prāṇāyāma by drilling the respiration; or by the jñānīs who try to find out the nondifferentiated Brahman by the process of elimination of the mundane, extending over thousands of millions of years.

PURPORT

The attainment of the lotus feet of Govinda consists in the realization of unalloyed devotion. The *kaivalya* (realized nonalternative state) which is attained by the *aṣṭāṅga-yogīs* by practicing trance for thousands of millions of years and the state of merging into the nondifferentiated impersonality of Godhead beyond the range of limitation attained by nondualists after a similar period passed in distinguishing between the spiritual and nonspiritual and eliminating things of the limited sphere one after another by the formula "not this, not that," are simply the outskirts of the lotus feet of Kṛṣṇa and not the lotus feet themselves. The long and short of the matter is this, *kaivalya* or merging into the Brahman constitutes the line of demarcation between the world of limitation and the transcendental world. For, unless we step beyond them, we can have no taste of the variegatedness of the transcendental sphere. These conditions are the simple absence of misery arising from mundane affinity but are not real happiness or felicity. If the absence of misery be called a bit of pleasure then also that bit is very small and of no consequence. It is not sufficient to destroy the condition of materiality; but the real gain to the *jīva* is his eternal existence in his self-realized state. This can be attained only by the grace of unalloyed devotion which is essentially *cit* or transcendental in character. For this end abstract and uninteresting mental speculation is of no avail.

TEXT 35

एकोऽप्यसौ रचयितुं जगदण्डकोटिं
यच्छक्तिरस्ति जगदण्डचया यदन्तः ।
अण्डान्तरस्थपरमाणुचयान्तरस्थं
गोविन्दमादिपुरुषं तमहं भजामि ॥३५॥

eko 'py asau racayituṁ jagad-aṇḍa-koṭiṁ
yac-chaktir asti jagad-aṇḍa-cayā yad-antaḥ
aṇḍāntara-stha-paramāṇu-cayāntara-sthaṁ
govindam ādi-puruṣaṁ tam ahaṁ bhajāmi

ekaḥ—one; *api*—although; *asau*—He; *racayitum*—to create; *jagat-aṇḍa*—of universes; *koṭim*—millions; *yat*—whose; *śaktiḥ*—potency; *asti*—there is; *jagat-aṇḍa-cayāḥ*—all the universes; *yat-antaḥ*—within whom; *aṇḍa-antara-stha*—which are scattered throughout the universe; *parama-aṇu-caya*—the atoms; *antara-stham*—situated within; *govindam*—Govinda; *ādi-puruṣam*—the original person; *tam*—Him; *aham*—I; *bhajāmi*—worship.

He is an undifferentiated entity as there is no distinction between potency and the possessor thereof. In His work of creation of millions of worlds, His potency remains inseparable. All the universes exist in Him and He is present in His fullness

in every one of the atoms that are scattered throughout the universe, at one and the same time. Such is the primeval Lord whom I adore.

PURPORT

Kṛṣṇa is the highest of all entities. In Him is an entity which is termed *cit* (spiritual) which is distinct from the principle of limitation. By His inconceivable power, He can at will create numberless universes. All the mundane universes owe their origin to the transformation of His external potency. Again His abode is beyond human conception; since all worlds, limited and spiritual (*cit*) exist in Him and He resides simultaneously in His fullness and entirety in all the atoms in all the worlds. All-pervasiveness is only a localized aspect of the majesty of Kṛṣṇa, the Lord of all. Though He is all-pervasive yet in His existence everywhere in a medium shape consists His spiritual Lordship beyond human conception. This argument favors the doctrine of simultaneous inconceivable distinction and nondistinction, and knocks down the contaminating Māyāvāda and other allied doctrines.

TEXT 36

यद्भावभावितधियो मनुजास्तथैव
सम्प्राप्य रूपमहिमासनयानभूषाः ।
सूक्तैर्यमेव निगमप्रथितैः स्तुवन्ति
गोविन्दमादिपुरुषं तमहं भजामि ॥३६॥

yad-bhāva-bhāvita-dhiyo manujās tathaiva
samprāpya rūpa-mahimāsana-yāna-bhūṣāḥ
sūktair yam eva nigama-prathitaiḥ stuvanti
govindam ādi-puruṣaṁ tam ahaṁ bhajāmi

yat—for whom; *bhāva*—with devotion; *bhāvita*—are imbued;

dhiyaḥ—whose hearts; *manujāḥ*—men; *tathā eva*—similarly; *samprāpya*—having gained; *rūpa*—beauty; *mahima*—greatness; *āsana*—thrones; *yāna*—conveyances; *bhūṣāḥ*—and ornaments; *sūktaiḥ*—by Vedic hymns; *yam*—whom; *eva*—certainly; *nigama*—by the *Vedas; prathitaiḥ*—told; *stuvanti*—offer praise; *govindam*—Govinda; *ādi-puruṣam*—the original person; *tam*—Him; *aham*—I; *bhajāmi*—worship.

I adore the same Govinda, the primeval Lord, in whose praise men, who are imbued with devotion, sing the mantra-sūktas told by the Vedas, by gaining their appropriate beauty, greatness, thrones, conveyances and ornaments.

PURPORT

In discussing *rasa* we meet with five kinds of devotion or service. *Śānta* or unattached, *dāsya* or pertaining to reverential willing service, *sakhya* or friendship, *vātsalya* or parental love and *śṛṅgāra* or juvenile love.

The devotees surcharged with the ideas of their respective service, serve Kṛṣṇa eternally and ultimately reach the goal of their respective ideals. They attain the real nature of their self befitting their respective *rasas*, their glories, conveyances, seats befitting their sacred service, and transcendental qualities of ornaments enhancing the beauty of their real nature. Those who are advocates of *śānta-rasa* attain the region of Brahma-Paramātmā, the seat of eternal peace; those of *dāsya-rasa* get to Vaikuṇṭha, the spiritual majestic abode of Śrī Nārāyaṇa; those of *sakhya, vātsalya and madhura-rasa* (juvenile love) attain Goloka-dhāma, Kṛṣṇa's abode, above Vaikuṇṭha. They worship Kṛṣṇa by the *sūktas* depicted in the *Vedas* with the ingredients and objects befitting their respective *rasas*, in those regions. The *Vedas*, under the influence of the spiritual potency in certain passages speak of the pastimes of the Supreme Lord. The liberated souls chant the name, qualities and pastimes of the Supreme

Lord, under the guidance of the same spiritual potency.

TEXT 37

आनन्दचिन्मयरसप्रतिभाविताभिस्
ताभिर्य एव निजरूपतया कलाभिः ।
गोलोक एव निवसत्यखिलात्मभूतो
गोविन्दमादिपुरुषं तमहं भजामि ॥३७॥

ānanda-cinmaya-rasa-pratibhāvitābhis
tābhir ya eva nija-rūpatayā kalābhiḥ
goloka eva nivasaty akhilātma-bhūto
govindam ādi-puruṣaṁ tam ahaṁ bhajāmi

ānanda—bliss; *cit*—and knowledge; *maya*—consisting of; *rasa*—mellows; *prati*—every second; *bhāvitābhiḥ*—who are engrossed with; *tābhiḥ*—with those; *yaḥ*—who; *eva*—certainly; *nija-rūpatayā*—with His own form; *kalābhiḥ*—who are parts of portions of His pleasure potency; *goloke*—in Goloka Vṛndāvana; *eva*—certainly; *nivasati*—resides; *akhila-ātma*—as the soul of all; *bhūtaḥ*—who exists; *govindam*—Govinda; *ādi-puruṣam*—the original personality; *tam*—Him; *aham*—I; *bhajāmi*—worship.

I worship Govinda, the primeval Lord, residing in His own realm, Goloka, with Rādhā, resembling His own spiritual figure, the embodiment of the ecstatic potency possessed of the sixty-four artistic activities, in the company of Her confidantes [sakhīs], embodiments of the extensions of Her bodily form, permeated and vitalized by His ever-blissful spiritual rasa.

PURPORT

Although the Lord Absolute and His potency are one and the self-same existence, still They exist eternally as separate entities, as Rādhā and Kṛṣṇa. In both the ecstatic energy and the transcendental Lord Kṛṣṇa, there exists *śṛṅgāra-rasa* (amorous love) whose quality is inconceivable. The *vibhāva* (extension) of that *rasa* (mellow quality) is twofold, viz., *ālambana* (prop) and *uddīpana* (stimulation). Of these *ālambana* is twofold, viz., *āśraya* (supported) and *viṣaya* (supporter). *Āśraya* signifies Rādhikā Herself and the extensions of Her own form and *viṣaya* means Kṛṣṇa Himself. Kṛṣṇa is Govinda, Lord of Goloka. The *gopīs* are the facsimile *āśraya* of that *rasa*. With them Kṛṣṇa indulges in eternal pastimes in Goloka. *Nija-rūpatayā* means "with the attributes manifested from the ecstatic energy." The sixty-four activities in fine arts and crafts are the following:

(1) *gīta*—art of singing. (2) *vādya*—art of playing on musical instruments. (3) *nṛtya*—art of dancing. (4) *nāṭya*—art of theatricals. (5) *ālekhya*—art of painting. (6) *viśeṣakacchedya*—art of painting the face and body with colored unguents and cosmetics. (7) *taṇḍula-kusuma-bali-vikāra*—art of preparing offerings from rice and flowers. (8) *puṣpāstaraṇa*—art of making a covering of flowers for a bed. (9) *daśana-vasanāṅga-rāga*—art of applying preparations for cleansing the teeth, cloths and painting the body. (10) *maṇi-bhūmikā-karma*—art of making the groundwork of jewels. (11) *śayyā-racana*—art of covering the bed. (12) *udaka-vādya*—art of playing on music in water. (13) *udaka-ghāta*—art of splashing with water. (14) *citra-yoga*—art of practically applying an admixture of colors. (15) *mālya-grathana-vikalpa*—art of designing a preparation of wreaths. (16) *śekharāpīḍa-yojana*—art of practically setting the coronet on the head. (17) *nepathya-yoga*—art of practically dressing in the tiring room. (18) *karṇapātra-bhaṅga*—art of decorating the tragus of the ear. (19) *sugandha-yukti*—art of practical application of aromatics. (20) *bhūṣaṇa-yojana*—art of applying or setting ornaments. (21) *aindra-jāla*—art of jugglery. (22) *kaucumāra*—a kind of art. (23) *hasta-lāghava*—art of sleight of hand. (24) *citra-śākāpūpa-bhakṣya-vikāra-kriyā*—art of preparing varieties of salad, bread, cake and delicious food. (25) *pānaka-rasa-rāgāsava-*

yojana—art of practically preparing palatable drinks and tinging draughts with red color. (26) *sūcī-vāya-karma*—art of needleworks and weaving. (27) *sūtra-krīḍā*—art of playing with thread. (28) *vīṇā-ḍamuraka-vādya*—art of playing on lute and small x-shaped drum. (29) *prahelikā*—art of making and solving riddles. (29a) *pratimālā*—art of caping or reciting verse for verse as a trial for memory or skill. (30) *durvacaka-yoga*—art of practicing language difficult to be answered by others. (31) *pustaka-vācana*—art of reciting books. (32) *nāṭikākhyāyikā-darśana*—art of enacting short plays and anecdotes. (33) *kāvya-samasyā-pūraṇa*—art of solving enigmatic verses. (34) *paṭṭikā-vetra-bāṇa-vikalpa*—art of designing preparation of shield, cane and arrows. (35) *tarku-karma*—art of spinning by spindle. (36) *takṣaṇa*—art of carpentry. (37) *vāstu-vidyā*—art of engineering. (38) *raupya-ratna-parīkṣā*—art of testing silver and jewels. (39) *dhātu-vāda*—art of metallurgy. (40) *maṇi-rāga jñāna*—art of tinging jewels. (41) *ākara jñāna*—art of mineralogy. (42) *vṛkṣāyur-veda-yoga*—art of practicing medicine or medical treatment, by herbs. (43) *meṣa-kukkuṭa-lāvaka-yuddha-vidhi*—art of knowing the mode of fighting of lambs, cocks and birds. (44) *śuka-śārikā-prapālana* (*pralāpana*)—art of maintaining or knowing conversation between male and female cockatoos. (45) *utsādana*—art of healing or cleaning a person with perfumes. (46) *keśa-mārjana-kauśala*—art of combing hair. (47) *akṣara-muṣṭikā-kathana*—art of talking with letters and fingers. (48) *mlecchita-kutarka-vikalpa*—art of fabricating barbarous or foreign sophistry. (49) *deśa-bhāṣā-jñāna*—art of knowing provincial dialects. (50) *puṣpa-śakaṭikā-nirmiti-jñāna*—art of knowing prediction by heavenly voice or knowing preparation of toy carts by flowers. (51) *yantra-māṭṛkā*—art of mechanics. (52) *dhāraṇa-māṭṛkā*—art of the use of amulets. (53) *samvācya*—art of conversation. (54) *mānasī kāvya-kriyā*—art of composing verse mentally. (55) *kriyā-vikalpa*—art of designing a literary work or a medical remedy. (56) *chalitaka-yoga*—art of practicing as a builder of shrines called after him. (57) *abhidhāna-koṣa-cchando-jñāna*—art of the use of lexicography and meters. (58) *vastra-gopana*—art of concealment of cloths. (59) *dyūta-viśeṣa*—art of knowing specific gambling. (60) *ākarṣa-krīḍā*—art of playing with dice or magnet. (61) *bālaka-krīḍanaka*—art of using children's toys. (62) *vaināyikī vidyā*—art of enforcing discipline. (63) *vaijayikī vidyā*—art of gaining victory. (64) *vaitālikī vidyā*—art of awakening master with music at dawn.

All these arts manifesting their own eternal forms are ever visible in the region of Goloka as the ingredients of *rasa;* and, in the mundane sphere, they have been unstintedly exhibited in the pastimes of Vraja by the spiritual (*cit*) potency, Yogamāyā. So Śrī Rūpa says, *sadānantaiḥ . . . santi tāḥ*, i.e., Kṛṣṇa is ever manifest in His beauty with His infinite pastimes in Goloka. Sometimes the variant manifestation of those pastimes becomes visible on the mundane plane. Śrī Hari, the Supreme Lord, also manifests His pastimes of birth, etc., accompanied by all His paraphernalia. The divine sportive potency fills the hearts of His paraphernalia with appropriate spiritual sentiments in conformity with the will of Kṛṣṇa. Those pastimes that manifest themselves on the mundane plane, are His *visible* pastimes. All those very pastimes exist in their nonvisible form in Goloka beyond the ken of mundane knowledge. In His visible pastimes Kṛṣṇa sojourns in Gokula, Mathurā and Dvārakā. Those pastimes that are nonvisible in those three places, are visible in their spiritual sites of Vṛndāvana.

From the conclusions just stated it is clear that there is no distinction between the visible and nonvisible pastimes. The apostle Jīva Gosvāmī in his commentary on this *śloka* as well as in the gloss of *Ujjvala-nīlamaṇi* and in *Kṛṣṇa-sandarbha* remarks that "the visible pastimes of Kṛṣṇa are the creation of His *cit* (spiritual) potency. Being in conjunction with the reference to mundane function they exhibit certain features which seem to be true by the influence of the limiting potency (Māyā); but these cannot exist in the transcendental reality. The destruction of demons, illicit paramourship, birth, etc., are examples of this peculiarity. The *gopīs* are the extensions of the ecstatic energy of Kṛṣṇa, and so are exceptionally His own. How can there be illicit connection in their case? The illicit mistress-ship of the *gopīs* found in His visible pastime, is but the mundane reflection of the transcendental reality." The hidden meaning underlying the words of Śrī Jīva Gosvāmī, when it is made explicit, will leave no doubt in the minds of the readers. Śrī Jīva Gosvāmī is our preacher of transcendental truth. So he is always under the influence of Śrī Rūpa and Sanātana. Moreover in the pastimes of Kṛṣṇa Śrī Jīva is one of the *mañjarīs*. So he is conversant with all transcendental realities.

There are some who, being unable to understand the drift of his statements, give meanings of their own invention and indulge in useless controversies. Śrī Rūpa and Sanātana say that there is no real and essential distinction between the *līlās* visible and nonvisible, the only distinction lies in this that one is manifest in the mundane sphere whereas the other is not so. In the supermundane manifestation there is absolute purity in the seer and the seen. A particularly fortunate person when he is favored by Kṛṣṇa, can shake off worldly shackles and connections, enter the transcendental region after attaining the realized taste of the varieties of *rasa* that is available during the period of novitiate. Only such a person can have a view and taste of the perfect and absolutely pure *līlā* of Goloka. Such receptive natures are rarely to be found. He, who exists in the mundane sphere, can also realize the taste of *cid-rasa* by the grace of Kṛṣṇa by being enabled to attain the realized state of service. Such a person can have a view of the pastimes of Goloka manifested in the mundane *līlā* of Gokula. There is certainly a difference between these two classes of eligible seekers of the truth. Until one attains the perfectly transcendental stage he must be hampered by his lingering limitations, in his vision of the pastimes of Goloka. Again, the vision of the transcendental reality varies according to the degree of self-realization. The vision of Goloka must also vary accordingly.

It is only those fettered souls who are excessively addicted to worldliness that are devoid of the devotional eye. Of them some are enmeshed by the variegatedness of the deluding energy while others aspire after self-annihilation under the influence of centrifugal knowledge. Though they might have a view of the mundanely manifested pastimes of the Supreme Lord, they can have only a material conception of those visible pastimes, this conception being devoid of transcendental reality. Hence the realization of Goloka appears in proportion to eligibility due to the degree of one's self-realization. The underlying principle is this, that, though Gokula is as holy and free from dross as Goloka, still it is manifested on the mundane plane by the influence of the *cit* potency, Yogamāyā. In visible and nonvisible matters of transcendental regions there is no impurity, contamination and imperfection inherent in the world of limitation; only there is some difference in the matter of realization in proportion to the self-realization of the seekers after the Absolute. Impurity, unwholesomeness, foreign elements, illusion, nescience, unholiness, utter inadequacy, insignificance, grossness—these appertain to the eye, intellect, mind and ego stultified by the material nature of conditioned souls; they have nothing to do with the essential nature of transcendence. The more one is free from these blots the more is one capable of realizing the unqualified Absolute. The truth who has been revealed by the scriptures, is free from dross. But the realizations of the seekers of the knowledge of these realities, are with or without flaw in accordance with the degree of their individual realization.

Those sixty-four arts that have been enumerated above, do in reality exist unstintedly only in Goloka. Unwholesomeness, insignificance, grossness are found in those arts in accordance with the degree of self-realization on the part of aspirants after the knowledge of the Absolute. According to Śrīla Rūpa and Śrīla Sanātana all those pastimes, that have been visible in Gokula, exist in all purity and free from all tinge of limitation in Goloka. So transcendental autocratic paramourship also exists in Goloka in inconceivable purity, judged by the same standard and reasoning. All manifestation by the *cit* potency, Yogamāyā, are pure. So, as the above paramourship is the creation of Yogamāyā, it is necessarily free from all contamination, and appertains to the absolute reality.

Let us pause to consider what the absolute reality is in Himself. Śrī Rūpa Gosvāmī says, *pūrvokta-. . . sārataḥ*. In regard to these *ślokas* Śrīpāda Jīva Gosvāmī after mature deliberation has established the transcendental paramourship as *vibhrama-vilāsa*, something seemingly different from what it appears to be; such are the pastimes of birth, etc., accomplished by Yogamāyā.

By the explanation *tathāpi . . . vraja-vanitānām*, Śrīla Jīva Gosvāmī has expressed his profound implication. Joyous pastimes by the medium of seeming error, *vibhrama-vilāsa*, as the contrivance of Yogamāyā, has also been admitted in the concluding statements of Rūpa and Sanātana. Still, since Śrīpāda Jīva Gosvāmī has established the identity of Goloka with Gokula, it must be admitted that there is transcendental reality underlying all the pastimes of Gokula. A husband is one who binds oneself in wedlock with a girl, while a paramour is one who, in order to win another's wife's love by means of love, crosses the conventions of morality, by the impulse of the sentiment that regards her love as the be-all and end-all of existence. In Goloka there is no such function at all as that of the nuptial relationship. Hence there is no husbandhood characterized by such connection. On the other hand since the *gopīs*, who are self-supported real entities are not tied to anybody else in wedlock, they cannot also have the state of concubinage. There can also be no separate entities in the forms of *svakīya* (conjugal) and *parakīya* (adulterous) states. In the visible pastimes on the mundane plane the function in the form of the nuptial relationship is found to exist. Kṛṣṇa is beyond the scope of that function. Hence the said function of the circle of all-love is contrived by Yogamāyā. Kṛṣṇa tastes the transcendental *rasa* akin to paramourship by overstepping that function. This pastime of going beyond the pale of the apparent moral function manifested by Yogamāyā, is, however, also observable only on the mundane plane by the eye that is enwrapped by the mundane covering; but there is really no such levity in the pastimes of Kṛṣṇa. The *rasa* of paramourship is certainly the extracted essence of all the *rasas*. If it be said that it does not exist in Goloka, it would be highly deprecatory to Goloka. It is not the fact that there is no supremely wholesome tasting of *rasa* in the supremely excellent realm of Goloka. Kṛṣṇa, the fountainhead of all *avatāras*, tastes the same in a distinct form in Goloka and in another distinct form in Gokula. Therefore, in spite of the seeming appearance, to the mundane eye, of outstepping the bounds of the legitimate function by the form of paramourship, there must be present the truth of it in some form even in Goloka. *Ātmārāmo 'py arīramat, ātmany avaruddha-sauratah, reme vraja-sundarībhir yathārbhakaḥ pratibimba-vibhramaḥ* and other texts of the scriptures go to show that self-delightedness is the essential distinctive quality of Kṛṣṇa Himself. Kṛṣṇa in His majestic *cit* realm causes the manifestation of His own *cit* potency as Lakṣmī and enjoys her as His own wedded consort. As this feeling of wedded consorthood preponderates there, *rasa* expands in a wholesome form only up to the state of servanthood (*dāsya-rasa*). But in Goloka He divides up His *cit* potency into thousands of *gopīs* and eternally engages in amorous pastimes with them by forgetting the sentiments of ownership. By the sentiments of ownership there cannot be the extreme inaccessibility of the *rasa*. So the *gopīs* have naturally, from eternity, the innate sentiment of being others' wedded wives. Kṛṣṇa too in response to that sentiment, by assuming the reciprocal sentiment of paramourship, performs the *rāsa* and the other amorous pastimes with the aid of the flute, His favorite *cher ami*. Goloka is the transcendental seat of eternally self-realized *rasa*, beyond limited conception. Hence in Goloka there is realization of the sentimental assumption of the *rasa* of paramourship.

Again such is the nature of the principle of the majesty that in the realm of Vaikuṇṭha there is no *rasa* of parental affection towards the source of all *avatāras*. But in Goloka, the seat of all superexcellent deliciousness, there is no more than the original sentimental egoistic assumption of the same *rasa*. There Nanda and Yaśodā are visibly present, but there is no occurrence of birth. For want of the occurrence of birth the assumed egoistic sentiment of parental affection of Nanda and Yaśodā has no foundation in the actual existence of such entities as father and mother, but it is of the nature of sentimental assumption on their parts, cf. *jayati jana-nivāso devakī-janma-vādaḥ*, etc. For the purpose of the realization of the *rasa* the assumed egoistic sentiment is, however, eternal. In the *rasa* of amorous love if the corresponding egoistic sentiments of concubinage and paramourship be mere eternal assumptions there is nothing to blame in them and it also does not go against the scriptures. When those transcendental entities of Goloka becomes manifest in Vraja then those two egoistic sentiments become somewhat more palpable to the mundane view in the phenomenal world and there comes to be this much difference only. In the *rasa* of parental affection the sentiments of Nanda and Yaśodā that they are parents becomes manifest in the more tangible form in the pastimes of birth etc., and in the amorous *rasa* the corresponding sentiments of concubinage in the respective *gopīs* become manifest in the forms of their marriages with Abhimanyu, Govardhana, etc. In reality there is no such separate entity as husbandhood of the *gopīs* either in Goloka or in Gokula. Hence the *śāstras* declare that there is no sexual union of the *gopīs* with their husbands. It is also for the same reason that the authorized teacher of the principle of *rasa*, Śrī Rūpa, writes that in the transcendental amorous *rasa* the hero is of two different types, viz., the wedded husband and the paramour—*patiś copapatiś ceti prabhedāv iha viśrutāv iti*. Śrī Jīva, in his commentary by his words *patiḥ pura-vanitānāṁ dvitīyo vraja-vanitānām*, acknowledges the eternal paramourship of Kṛṣṇa in Goloka and Gokula and the husbandhood of Kṛṣṇa in Vaikuṇṭha and Dvārakā etc. In the Lord of Goloka and the Lord of Gokula the character of paramourship is found in its complete form. Kṛṣṇa's deliberate overstepping of His own quality of self-delightedness is caused by the desire of union with another's wedded wife. The state of being another's wedded wife is nothing but the corresponding assumed sentiment on the part of the *gopīs*. In reality they have no husbands with independent and separate existence; still their very egoistic sentiment makes them have the nature of the wedded wives of others. So all the characteristics, viz., that "desire makes the paramour overstep the bounds of duty," etc., are eternally present in the seat of all "deliciousness." In Vraja that very thing reveals itself, to an extent, in a form more tangible to persons with mundane eyes.

So in Goloka there is inconceivable distinction and nondistinction between the *rasas* analogous to mundane concubineship and wifehood. It may be said with equal truth that there is no distinction in Goloka between the two as also that there is such distinction. The essence of paramourship is the cessation of ownership and the abeyance of ownership is the enjoyment of His own *cit* potency in the shape of abeyance of paramourship or enjoyment without the sanction of wedlock. The conjunction of the two exists there as one *rasa* accommodating both varieties. In Gokula it is really the same with the difference that it produces a different impression on observers belonging to the mundane plane. In Govinda, the hero of Goloka, there exist both husbandhood and paramourship above all piety and impiety and free from all grossness. Such is also the case with the hero of Gokula although there is a distinction in realization caused by Yogamāyā. If it be urged that what is manifested by Yogamāyā is the highest truth being the creation of the *cit* potency and that, therefore, the impression of paramourship is also really true, the reply is that there may exist an impression of analogous sentimental egoism in the tasting of *rasa* free from any offense because it is not without a basis in truth. But the unwholesome impression that is produced in the mundane judgment is offensive and as such cannot exist in the pure *cit* realm. In fact Śrīpāda Jīva Gosvāmī has come to the true conclusion, and at the same time the finding of the opposing party is also inconceivably true. It is the vain empirical wranglings about wedded wifehood and concubinage which is false and full of specious verbosity. He who goes through the commentaries of Śrīpāda Jīva Gosvāmī and those of the opposing party with an impartial judgment cannot maintain his attitude of protest engendered by any real doubt. What the unalloyed devotee of the Supreme Lord says is all true and is independent of any consideration of unwholesome pros and cons. There is, however, the element of mystery in their verbal controversies. Those, whose judgment is made of mundane stuff, being unable to enter into the spirit of the all-loving controversies among pure devotees, due to their own want of unalloyed devotion, are apt to impute to the devotees their own defects of partisanship and opposing views. Commenting on the *śloka* of *Rāsa-pañcādhyāyī, gopīnāṁ tat-patīnāṁ ca*, etc., what Śrīpāda Sanātana Gosvāmī has stated conclusively in his *Vaiṣṇava-toṣaṇī* has been accepted with reverence by the true devotee Śrīpāda Viśvanātha Cakravartī without any protest.

Whenever any dispute arises regarding the pure cognitive pastimes, such as Goloka, etc., we would do well to remember the precious advice from the holy lips of Śrīmān Mahāprabhu and His associates, the Gosvāmīs, viz., that the Truth Absolute is ever characterized by spiritual variegatedness that transcends the variegatedness of mundane phenomena; but He is *never* featureless. The divine *rasa* is lovely with the variegatedness of the fourfold distinction of *vibhāva*, *anubhāva*, *sāttvika* and *vyabhicārī* and the *rasa* is ever present in Goloka and Vaikuṇṭha. The *rasa* of Goloka manifests as *vraja-rasa* on the mundane plane for the benefit of the devotees by the power of Yogamāyā. Whatever is observable in *gokula-rasa* should be visible in *goloka-rasa*, in a clearly explicit form. Hence the distinction of paramourship and concubinage, the variegatedness of the respective *rasas* of all different persons, the soil, water, river, hill, portico, bower, cows, etc., all the features of Gokula exist in Goloka, disposed in an appropriate manner. There is only this peculiarity that the mundane conceptions of human beings possessed of material judgment, regarding those transcendental entities, do not exist there. The conception of Goloka manifests itself differently in proportion to the degree of realization of the various pastimes of Vraja and it is very difficult to lay down any definite criterion as to which portions are mundane and which are uncontaminated. The more the eye of devotion is tinged with the salve of love, the more will the transcendental concept gradually manifest itself. So there is no need of further hypothetical speculation which does not improve one's spiritual appreciation, as the substantive knowledge of Goloka is an inconceivable entity. To try to pursue the inconceivable by the conceptual process is like pounding the empty husk of grain, which is sure to have a fruitless ending. It is, therefore, one's bounden duty, by refraining from the endeavor to know, to try to gain the experience of the transcendental by the practice of pure devotion. Any course, the adoption of which tends to produce the impression of featurelessness, must be shunned by all means. Unalloyed *parakīya-rasa* free from all mundane conception is a most rare attainment. It is this which has been described in the narrative of the pastimes of Gokula. Those devotees, who follow the dictate of their pure spontaneous love, should base their devotional endeavors on that narrative. They will attain to the more wholesome fundamental principle on reaching the stage of realization. The devotional activities characterized by illicit amour, as practiced by worldly-minded conditioned souls, are forbidden mundane impiety. The heart of our apostle Śrīpāda Jīva Gosvāmī was very much moved by such practices and induced him to give us his conclusive statements on the subject. It is the duty of a pure Vaiṣṇava to accept the real spirit of his statements. It is a great offense to disrespect the *ācārya* and to seek to establish a different doctrine in opposition to him.

TEXT 38

प्रेमाञ्जनच्छुरितभक्तिविलोचनेन
सन्तः सदैव हृदयेषु विलोकयन्ति ।
यं श्यामसुन्दरमचिन्त्यगुणस्वरूपं
गोविन्दमादिपुरुषं तमहं भजामि ॥३८॥

premāñjana-cchurita-bhakti-vilocanena
santaḥ sadaiva hṛdayeṣu vilokayanti
yaṁ śyāmasundaram acintya-guṇa-svarūpaṁ
govindam ādi-puruṣaṁ tam ahaṁ bhajāmi

prema—of love; *añjana*—with the salve; *churita*—tinged; *bhakti*—of devotion; *vilocanena*—with the eye; *santaḥ*—the pure devotees; *sadā*—always; *eva*—indeed; *hṛdayeṣu*—in their hearts; *vilokayanti*—see; *yam*—whom; *śyāma*—dark blue; *sundaram*—beautiful; *acintya*—inconceivable; *guṇa*—with attributes; *svarūpam*—whose nature is endowed; *govindam*—Govinda; *ādi-puruṣam*—the original person; *tam*—Him; *aham*—I; *bhajāmi*—worship.

I worship Govinda, the primeval Lord, who is Śyāmasundara, Kṛṣṇa Himself with inconceivable innumerable attributes, whom the pure devotees see in their heart of hearts with the eye of devotion tinged with the salve of love.

PURPORT

The Śyāmasundara form of Kṛṣṇa is His inconceivable simultaneous personal and impersonal self-contradictory form. True devotees see that form in their purified hearts under the influence of devotional trance. The form Śyāma is not the blue color visible in the mundane world but is the transcendental variegated color affording eternal bliss, and is not visible to the mortal eye. On a consideration of the trance of Vyāsadeva as in the *śloka*, *bhakti-yogena manasi* etc., it will be clear that the form of Śrī Kṛṣṇa is the full Personality of Godhead and can only be visible in the heart of a true devotee, which is the only true seat in the state of trance under the influence of devotion. When Kṛṣṇa manifested Himself in Vraja, both the devotees and nondevotees saw Him with this very eye; but only the devotees cherished Him, eternally present in Vraja, as the priceless jewel of their heart. Nowadays also the devotees see Him in Vraja in their hearts, saturated with devotion although they do not see Him with their eyes. The eye of devotion is nothing but the eye of the pure unalloyed spiritual self of the *jīva*. The form of Kṛṣṇa is visible to that eye in proportion to its purification by the practice of devotion. When the devotion of the neophyte reaches the stage of *bhāva-bhakti* the pure eye of that devotee is tinged with the salve of love by the grace of Kṛṣṇa, which enables him to see Kṛṣṇa face to face. The phrase "in their hearts" means Kṛṣṇa is visible in proportion as their hearts are purified by the practice of devotion. The sum and substance of this *śloka* is that the form of Kṛṣṇa, who is Śyāmasundara, Naṭavara (Best Dancer), Muralīdhara (Holder of the Flute) and Tribhaṅga (Triple-bending), is not a mental concoction but is transcendental, and is visible with the eye of the soul of the devotee under trance.

TEXT 39

रामादिमूर्तिषु कलानियमेन तिष्ठन्
नानावतारमकरोद्भुवनेषु किन्तु ।
कृष्णः स्वयं समभवत्परमः पुमान् यो
गोविन्दमादिपुरुषं तमहं भजामि ॥३९॥

rāmādi-mūrtiṣu kalā-niyamena tiṣṭhan
nānāvatāram akarod bhuvaneṣu kintu
kṛṣṇaḥ svayaṁ samabhavat paramaḥ pumān yo
govindam ādi-puruṣaṁ tam ahaṁ bhajāmi

rāma-ādi—the incarnation of Lord Rāma, etc.; *mūrtiṣu*—in different forms; *kalā-niyamena*—by the order of plenary portions; *tiṣṭhan*—existing; *nānā*—various; *avatāram*—incarnations; *akarot*—executed; *bhuvaneṣu*—within the worlds; *kintu*—but; *kṛṣṇaḥ*—Lord Kṛṣṇa; *svayam*—personally; *samabhavat*—appeared; *paramaḥ*—the supreme; *pumān*—person; *yaḥ*—who; *govindam*—Govinda; *ādi-puruṣam*—the original person; *tam*—Him; *aham*—I; *bhajāmi*—worship.

I worship Govinda, the primeval Lord, who manifested Himself personally as Kṛṣṇa and the different avatāras in the world in the forms of Rāma, Nṛsiṁha, Vāmana, etc., as His subjective portions.

PURPORT

His subjective portions as the *avatāras*, viz., Rāma, etc., appear from Vaikuṇṭha and His own form Kṛṣṇa manifests Himself with Vraja in this world, from Goloka. The underlying sense is that Kṛṣṇa Caitanya, identical with Kṛṣṇa Himself, also brings about by His appearance the direct manifestation of Godhead Himself.

TEXT 40

यस्य प्रभा प्रभवतो जगदण्डकोटि-
कोटिष्वशेषवसुधादि विभूतिभिन्नम् ।
तद् ब्रह्म निष्कलमनन्तमशेषभूतं
गोविन्दमादिपुरुषं तमहं भजामि ॥४०॥

yasya prabhā prabhavato jagad-aṇḍa-koṭi-
koṭiṣv aśeṣa-vasudhādi vibhūti-bhinnam
tad brahma niṣkalam anantam aśeṣa-bhūtaṁ
govindam ādi-puruṣaṁ tam ahaṁ bhajāmi

yasya—of whom; *prabhā*—the effulgence; *prabhavataḥ*—of one who excels in power; *jagat-aṇḍa*—of universes; *koṭi-koṭiṣu*—in millions and millions; *aśeṣa*—unlimited; *vasudhā-ādi*—with planets and other manifestations; *vibhūti*—with opulences; *bhinnam*—becoming variegated; *tat*—that; *brahma*—Brahman; *niṣkalam*—without parts; *anantam*—unlimited; *aśeṣa-bhūtam*—being complete; *govindam*—Govinda; *ādi-puruṣam*—the original person; *tam*—Him; *aham*—I; *bhajāmi*—worship.

I worship Govinda, the primeval Lord, whose effulgence is the source of the nondifferentiated Brahman mentioned in the Upaniṣads, being differentiated from the infinity of glories of the mundane universe appears as the indivisible, infinite, limitless, truth.

PURPORT

The mundane universe created by Māyā is one of the infinite external manifestations accommodating space, time and gross things. The impersonal aspect of Godhead, the nondifferentiated Brahman, is far above this principle of mundane creation. But even the nondifferentiated Brahman is only the external effulgence emanating from the boundary wall of the transcendental realm of Vaikuṇṭha displaying the triquadrantal glory of Govinda. The nondifferentiated Brahman is indivisible, hence is also one without a second, and is the infinite, and residual entity.

TEXT 41

माया हि यस्य जगदण्डशतानि सूते
त्रैगुण्यतद्विषयवेदवितायमाना ।
सत्त्वावलम्बिपरसत्त्वं विशुद्धसत्त्वं
गोविन्दमादिपुरुषं तमहं भजामि ॥४१॥

māyā hi yasya jagad-aṇḍa-śatāni sūte
traiguṇya-tad-viṣaya-veda-vitāyamānā
sattvāvalambi-para-sattvaṁ viśuddha-sattvaṁ
govindam ādi-puruṣaṁ tam ahaṁ bhajāmi

māyā—the external potency; *hi*—indeed; *yasya*—of whom; *jagat-aṇḍa*—of universes; *śatāni*—hundreds; *sūte*—brings forth; *trai-guṇya*—embodying the threefold mundane qualities; *tat*—of that; *viṣaya*—the subject matter; *veda*—the Vedic knowledge; *vitāyamānā*—diffusing; *sattva-avalambi*—the support of all existence; *para-sattvam*—the ultimate entity; *viśuddha-sattvam*—the absolute substantive principle; *govindam*—Govinda; *ādi-puruṣam*—the original person; *tam*—Him; *aham*—I; *bhajāmi*—worship.

I worship Govinda, the primeval Lord, who is the absolute substantive principle being the ultimate entity in the form of the support of all existence whose external potency embodies the threefold mundane qualities, viz., sattva, rajas and tamas and diffuses the Vedic knowledge regarding the mundane world.

PURPORT

The active mundane quality of *rajas* brings forth or generates all mundane entities. The quality of *sattva* (mundane manifestive principle) in conjunction with *rajas* stands for the maintenance of the existence of entities that are so produced, and the quality of *tamas* represents the principle of destruction. The substantive principle, which is mixed with the threefold mundane qualities, is mundane, while the unmixed substance is transcendental. The quality of eternal existence is the principle of absolute entity. The person whose proper form abides in that essence, is alone unalloyed entity, nonmundane, supermundane and free from all mundane quality. He is cognitive bliss. It is the deluding energy who has elaborated the regulative knowledge (*Vedas*) bearing on the threefold mundane quality.

TEXT 42

आनन्दचिन्मयरसात्मतया मनःसु
  यः प्राणिनां प्रतिफलन् स्मरतामुपेत्य ।
लीलायितेन भुवनानि जयत्यजस्रं
  गोविन्दमादिपुरुषं तमहं भजामि ॥४२॥

ānanda-cinmaya-rasātmatayā manaḥsu
  yaḥ prāṇināṁ pratiphalan smaratām upetya
līlāyitena bhuvanāni jayaty ajasraṁ
  govindam ādi-puruṣaṁ tam ahaṁ bhajāmi

ānanda—blissful; *cit-maya*—cognitive; *rasa*—of *rasa; ātma-tayā*—due to being the entity; *manaḥsu*—in the minds; *yaḥ*—He who; *prāṇinām*—of living entities; *pratiphalan*—being reflected; *smaratām upetya*—recollecting; *līlāyitena*—by pastimes; *bhu-vanāni*—the mundane world; *jayati*—triumphantly dominates; *ajasram*—ever; *govindam*—Govinda; *ādi-puruṣam*—the original person; *tam*—Him; *aham*—I; *bhajāmi*—worship.

I worship Govinda, the primeval Lord, whose glory ever triumphantly dominates the mundane world by the activity of His own pastimes, being reflected in the mind of recollecting souls

as the transcendental entity of ever-blissful cognitive rasa.

PURPORT

Those who constantly recollect in accordance with spiritual instructions the name, figure, attributes and pastimes of the form of Kṛṣṇa appearing in the amorous *rasa*, whose loveliness vanquishes the god of mundane love, conqueror of all mundane hearts, are alone meditators of Kṛṣṇa. Kṛṣṇa, who is full of pastimes, always manifests Himself with His realm only in the pure receptive cognition of such persons. The pastimes of that manifested divine realm triumphantly dominates in every way all the majesty and beauty of the mundane world.

TEXT 43

गोलोकनाम्नि निजधाम्नि तले च तस्य
देवीमहेशहरिधामसु तेषु तेषु ।
ते ते प्रभावनिचया विहिताश्च येन
गोविन्दमादिपुरुषं तमहं भजामि ॥४३॥

goloka-nāmni nija-dhāmni tale ca tasya
devī-maheśa-hari-dhāmasu teṣu teṣu
te te prabhāva-nicayā vihitāś ca yena
govindam ādi-puruṣaṁ tam ahaṁ bhajāmi

goloka-nāmni—in the planet known as Goloka Vṛndāvana; *nija-dhāmni*—the personal abode of the Supreme Personality of Godhead; *tale*—in the part underneath; *ca*—also; *tasya*—of that; *devī*—of the goddess Durgā; *maheśa*—of Lord Śiva; *hari*—of Nārāyaṇa; *dhāmasu*—in the planets; *teṣu teṣu*—in each of them; *te te*—those respective; *prabhāva-nicayāḥ*—opulences; *vihitāḥ*—established; *ca*—also; *yena*—by whom; *govindam*—Govinda; *ādi-puruṣam*—the original per-

His Divine Grace
Bhaktisiddhānta Sarasvatī Gosvāmī Ṭhākura
(1874–1937)
Founder of the Gaudiya Math and author of this
Brahma-saṁhitā translation and commentary

His Divine Grace
A. C. Bhaktivedanta Swami Prabhupāda
(1896–1977)
Founder-*Ācārya* of the International Society for Krishna Consciousness and foremost disciple of Bhaktisiddhānta Sarasvatī

Lord Caitanya Mahāprabhu

A full incarnation of the Supreme Personality of Godhead, Lord Kṛṣṇa, He appeared five hundred twenty-five years ago in India. In the early part of the sixteenth century He discovered the manuscript of the *Brahma-saṁhitā*.

The Ādi-Keśava temple, in southern India's Travancore state, where Lord Caitanya discovered the manuscript of the *Brahma-saṁhitā*. While there He discussed spiritual matters among highly advanced devotees.

Brahmā is the creator of the universe. Inspired by the Supreme Lord, he manifests the varieties of living entities, the arts and sciences, and the states of ignorance and enlightenment. His hymns in praise of Lord Kṛṣṇa constitute the *Brahma-saṁhitā*.

"Kṛṣṇa, who is known as Govinda, is the Supreme Godhead. He has an eternal, blissful, spiritual body. He is the origin of all. He has no other origin, and He is the prime cause of all causes."

—*Brahma-saṁhitā* 1

"I worship Govinda, the primeval Lord, residing in His own realm, Goloka, with Rādhā, resembling His own spiritual figure, the embodiment of the ecstatic potency possessed of the sixty-four artistic activities."

—*Brahma-saṁhitā* 37

"I worship that transcendental seat, known as Śvetadvīpa, where as loving consorts the Lakṣmīs in their unalloyed spiritual essence practice the amorous service of the Supreme Lord Kṛṣṇa as their only lover."

—*Brahma-saṁhitā* 56

son; *tam*—Him; *aham*—I; *bhajāmi*—worship.

Lowest of all is located Devī-dhāma [mundane world], next above it is Maheśa-dhāma [abode of Maheśa]; above Maheśa-dhāma is placed Hari-dhāma [abode of Hari] and above them all is located Kṛṣṇa's own realm named Goloka. I adore the primeval Lord Govinda, who has allotted their respective authorities to the rulers of those graded realms.

PURPORT

The realm of Goloka stands highest above all others. Brahmā looking up to the higher position of Goloka is speaking of the other realms from the point of view of his own realm: the first in order is this mundane world called Devī-dhāma consisting of the fourteen worlds, viz., Satyaloka, etc.; next above Devī-dhāma is located Śiva-dhāma one portion of which, called Mahākāla-dhāma, is enveloped in darkness; interpenetrating this portion of Śiva-dhāma there shines the Sadāśivaloka, full of great light. Above the same appears Hari-dhāma or the transcendental Vaikuṇṭhaloka. The potency of Devī-dhāma, in the form of the extension of Māyā, and that of Śivaloka, consisting of time, space and matter, are the potency of the separated particles pervaded by the penumbral reflection of the subjective portion of the Divinity. But Hari-dhāma is ever resplendent with transcendental majesty and the great splendor of all-sweetness predominates over all other majesties in Goloka. The Supreme Lord Govinda by his own direct and indirect power has constituted those respective potencies of those realms.

TEXT 44

सृष्टिस्थितिप्रलयसाधनशक्तिरेका
छायेव यस्य भुवनानि बिभर्ति दुर्गा ।

इच्छानुरूपमपि यस्य च चेष्टते सा
गोविन्दमादिपुरुषं तमहं भजामि ॥४४॥

sṛṣṭi-sthiti-pralaya-sādhana-śaktir ekā
chāyeva yasya bhuvanāni bibharti durgā
icchānurūpam api yasya ca ceṣṭate sā
govindam ādi-puruṣaṁ tam ahaṁ bhajāmi

sṛṣṭi—creation; *sthiti*—preservation; *pralaya*—and destruction; *sādhana*—the agency; *śaktiḥ*—potency; *ekā*—one; *chāyā*—the shadow; *iva*—like; *yasya*—of whom; *bhuvanāni*—the mundane world; *bibharti*—maintains; *durgā*—Durgā; *icchā*—the will; *anu-rūpam*—in accordance with; *api*—certainly; *yasya*—of whom; *ca*—and; *ceṣṭate*—conducts herself; *sā*—she; *govindam*—Govinda; *ādi-puruṣam*—the original person; *tam*—Him; *aham*—I; *bhajāmi*—worship.

The external potency Māyā who is of the nature of the shadow of the cit potency, is worshiped by all people as Durgā, the creating, preserving and destroying agency of this mundane world. I adore the primeval Lord Govinda in accordance with whose will Durgā conducts herself.

PURPORT

(The aforesaid presiding deity of Devī-dhāma is being described.) The world, in which Brahmā takes his stand and hymns the Lord of Goloka, is Devī-dhāma consisting of the fourteen worlds and Durgā is its presiding deity. She is ten-armed, representing the tenfold fruitive activities. She rides on the lion, representing her heroic prowess. She tramples down Mahīṣāsura, representing the subduer of vices. She is the mother of two sons, Kārttikeya and Gaṇeśa, representing beauty and success. She is placed between Lakṣmī and Sarasvatī, representing mundane opulence and mundane knowledge. She is armed with the twenty weapons, representing the various pious activities enjoined by the *Vedas* for suppression of vices. She holds the snake, representing the beauty of destructive time. Such is Durgā possessing all these manifold forms. Durgā is possessed of *durga*, which means a prison house. When *jīvas* begotten of the marginal potency (*taṭasthā śakti*) forget the service of Kṛṣṇa they are confined in the mundane prison house, the citadel of Durgā. The wheel of *karma* is the instrument of punishment at this place. The work of purifying these penalized *jīvas* is the duty devolved upon Durgā. She is incessantly engaged in discharging the same by the will of Govinda. When, luckily, the forgetfulness of Govinda on the part of imprisoned *jīvas* is remarked by them by coming in contact with self-realized souls and their natural aptitude for the loving service of Kṛṣṇa is aroused, Durgā herself then becomes the agency of their deliverance by the will of Govinda. So it behooves everybody to obtain the guileless grace of Durgā, the mistress of this prison house, by propitiating her with the selfless service of Kṛṣṇa. The boons received from Durgā in the shape of wealth, property, recovery from illness, of wife and sons, should be realized as the deluding kindness of Durgā. The mundane psychical jubilations of *daśa-mahā-vidyā*, the ten goddesses or forms of Durgā, are elaborated for the delusion of the fettered souls of this world. *Jīva* is a spiritual atomic part of Kṛṣṇa. When he forgets his service of Kṛṣṇa he is at once deflected by the attracting power of Māyā in this world, who throws him into the whirlpool of mundane fruitive activity (*karma*) by confining him in a gross body constituted by the five material elements, their five attributes and eleven senses, resembling the garb of a prisoner. In this whirlpool *jīva* has experience of happiness and miseries, heaven and hell. Besides this, there is a subtle body, consisting of the mind, intelligence and ego, inside the gross body. By means of the subtle body, the *jīva* forsakes one gross body and takes recourse to another. The *jīva* cannot get rid of the subtle body, full of nescience and evil desires, unless and until he is liberated. On getting rid of the subtle body he bathes in the Virajā and goes up to Hari-dhāma. Such are the duties performed by Durgā in accordance with the will of Govinda. In the *Bhāgavata śloka*, *vilajyamānayā . . . durdhiyaḥ*—the relationship between Durgā and the conditioned souls has been described.

Durgā, worshiped by the people of this mundane world, is the Durgā described above. But the *spiritual* Durgā, mentioned in the *mantra* which is the outer covering of the spiritual realm of the Supreme Lord, is the eternal maidservant of Kṛṣṇa and is, therefore, the transcendental reality whose shadow, the Durgā of this world, functions in this mundane world as her maidservant. (*Vide* the purport of *śloka* 3.)

TEXT 45

क्षीरं यथा दधि विकारविशेषयोगात्
सञ्जायते न हि ततः पृथगस्ति हेतोः ।
यः शम्भुतामपि तथा समुपैति कार्याद्
गोविन्दमादिपुरुषं तमहं भजामि ॥४५॥

kṣīraṁ yathā dadhi vikāra-viśeṣa-yogāt
sañjāyate na hi tataḥ pṛthag asti hetoḥ
yaḥ śambhutām api tathā samupaiti kāryād
govindam ādi-puruṣaṁ tam ahaṁ bhajāmi

kṣīram—milk; *yathā*—as; *dadhi*—yogurt; *vikāra-viśeṣa*—of a special transformation; *yogāt*—by the application; *sañjāyate*—is transformed into; *na*—not; *hi*—indeed; *tataḥ*—from the milk; *pṛthak*—separated; *asti*—is; *hetoḥ*—which is the cause; *yaḥ*—who; *śambhutām*—the nature of Lord Śiva; *api*—also; *tathā*—thus; *samupaiti*—accepts; *kāryāt*—for the matter of some particular business; *govindam*—Govinda; *ādi-puruṣam*—the original person; *tam*—Him; *aham*—I; *bhajāmi*—worship.

Just as milk is transformed into curd by the action of acids, but yet the effect curd is neither same as, nor different from, its cause, viz., milk, so I adore the primeval Lord Govinda of whom the state of Śambhu is a transformation for the performance of the work of destruction.

PURPORT

(The real nature of Śambhu, the presiding deity of Maheśa-dhāma, is described.) Śambhu is not a second Godhead other than Kṛṣṇa. Those, who entertain such discriminating sentiment, commit a great offense against the Supreme Lord. The supremacy of Śambhu is subservient to that of Govinda; hence they are not really different from each other. The nondistinction is established by the fact that just as milk treated with acid turns into curd so Godhead becomes a subservient when He Himself attains a distinct personality by the addition of a particular element of adulteration. This personality has no independent initiative. The said adulterating principle is constituted of a combination of the stupefying quality of the deluding energy, the quality of nonplenitude of the marginal potency and a slight degree of the ecstatic-cum-cognitive principle of the plenary spiritual potency. This specifically adulterated reflection of the principle of the subjective portion of the Divinity is Sadāśiva, in the form of the effulgent masculine-symbol-god Śambhu from whom Rudradeva is manifested. In the work of mundane creation as the material cause, in the work of preservation by the destruction of sundry *asuras* and in the work of destruction to conduct the whole operation, Govinda manifests Himself as *guṇa-avatāra* in the form of Śambhu who is the separated portion of Govinda imbued with the principle of His subjective plenary portion. The personality of the destructive principle in the form of time has been identified with that of Śambhu by scriptural evidences that have been adduced in the commentary. The purport of the *Bhāgavata ślokas*, viz., *vaiṣṇavānāṁ yathā śambhuḥ*, etc., is that Śambhu, in pursuance of the will of Govinda, works in union with his consort Durgādevī by his own time energy. He teaches pious duties (*dharma*) as stepping-stones to the attainment of spiritual service in the various *tantra-śāstras*, etc., suitable for *jīvas* in different grades of the conditional existence. In obedience to the will of Govinda, Śambhu maintains and fosters the religion of pure devotion by preaching the cult of illusionism (Māyāvāda) and the speculative *āgama-śāstras*. The fifty attributes of individual souls are manifest in a far vaster measure in Śambhu and five additional attributes not attainable by *jīvas* are also partly found in him. So Śambhu cannot be called a *jīva*. He is the lord of *jīva* but yet partakes of the nature of a *separated* portion of Govinda.

TEXT 46

दीपार्चिरेव हि दशान्तरमभ्युपेत्य
दीपायते विवृतहेतुसमानधर्मा ।
यस्तादृगेव हि च विष्णुतया विभाति
गोविन्दमादिपुरुषं तमहं भजामि ॥४६॥

dīpārcir eva hi daśāntaram abhyupetya
dīpāyate vivṛta-hetu-samāna-dharmā
yas tādṛg eva hi ca viṣṇutayā vibhāti
govindam ādi-puruṣaṁ tam ahaṁ bhajāmi

dīpa-arciḥ—the flame of a lamp; *eva*—as; *hi*—certainly; *daśā-antaram*—another lamp; *abhyupetya*—expanding; *dīpāyate*—illuminates; *vivṛta-hetu*—with its expanded cause; *samāna-dharmā*—equally powerful; *yaḥ*—who; *tādṛk*—similarly; *eva*—indeed; *hi*—certainly; *ca*—also; *viṣṇutayā*—by His expansion as Lord Viṣṇu; *vibhāti*—illuminates; *govindam*—

Govinda; *ādi-puruṣam*—the original person; *tam*—Him; *aham*—I; *bhajāmi*—worship.

The light of one candle being communicated to other candles, although it burns separately in them, is the same in its quality. I adore the primeval Lord Govinda who exhibits Himself equally in the same mobile manner in His various manifestations.

PURPORT

The presiding Deities of Hari-dhāma, viz., Hari, Nārāyaṇa, Viṣṇu, etc., the subjective portions of Kṛṣṇa, are being described. The majestic manifestation of Kṛṣṇa is Nārāyaṇa, Lord of Vaikuṇṭha, whose subjective portion is Kāraṇodakaśāyī Viṣṇu, the prime cause, whose portion is Garbhodakaśāyī. Kṣīrodakaśāyī is again the subjective portion of Garbhodakaśāyī Viṣṇu. The word "Viṣṇu" indicates all-pervading, omnipresent and omniscient personality. In this *śloka* the activities of the subjective portions of the Divinity are enunciated by the specification of the nature of Kṣīrodakaśāyī Viṣṇu. The personality of Viṣṇu, the embodied form of the manifestive quality (*sattva-guṇa*) is quite distinct from that of Śambhu who is adulterated with mundane qualities. Viṣṇu's subjective personality is on a level with that of Govinda. Both consist of the unadulterated substantive principle. Viṣṇu in the form of the manifest causal principle is identical with Govinda as regards quality. The manifestive quality (*sattva-guṇa*) that is found to exist in the triple mundane quality, is an adulterated entity, being alloyed with the qualities of mundane activity and inertia. Brahmā is the dislocated portion of the Divinity, manifested in the principle of mundane action, endowed with the functional nature of His subjective portion; and Śambhu is the dislocated portion of the Divinity manifested in the principle of mundane inertia possessing similarly the functional nature of His subjective portion. The reason for their being dislocated portions is that the two principles of mundane action and inertia being altogether wanting in the spiritual essence any entities, that are manifested in them, are located at a great distance from the Divinity Himself or His facsimiles. Although the mundane manifestive quality is of the adulterated kind, Viṣṇu, the manifestation of the Divinity in the mundane manifestive quality, makes His appearance in the unadulterated manifestive principle which is a constituent of the mundane manifestive quality. Hence Viṣṇu is the full subjective portion and belongs to the category of the superior *īśvaras*. He is the Lord of the deluding potency and not alloyed with her. Viṣṇu is the agent of Govinda's own subjective nature in the form of the prime cause. All the majestic attributes of Govinda, aggregating sixty in number, are fully present in His majestic manifestation, Nārāyaṇa. Brahmā and Śiva are entities adulterated with mundane qualities. Though Viṣṇu is also divine appearance in mundane quality (*guṇa-avatāra*), still He is not adulterated. The appearance of Nārāyaṇa in the form of Mahā-Viṣṇu, the appearance of Mahā-Viṣṇu in the form of Garbhodakaśāyī and the appearance of Viṣṇu in the form of Kṣīrodakaśāyī, are examples of the ubiquitous function of the Divinity. Viṣṇu is Godhead Himself, and the two other *guṇa-avatāras* and all the other gods are entities possessing authority in subordination to Him. From the subjective majestic manifestation of the supreme self-luminous Govinda emanate Kāraṇodakaśāyī, Garbhodakaśāyī, Kṣīrodakaśāyī and all other derivative subjective divine descents (*avatāras*) such as Rāma, etc., analogous to communicated light appearing in different candles, shining by the operation of the spiritual potency of Govinda.

TEXT 47

यः कारणार्णवजले भजति स्म योग-
निद्रामनन्तजगदण्डसरोमकूपः ।
आधारशक्तिमवलम्ब्य परां स्वमूर्तिं
गोविन्दमादिपुरुषं तमहं भजामि ॥४७॥

yaḥ kāraṇārṇava-jale bhajati sma yoga-
nidrām ananta-jagad-aṇḍa-sa-roma-kūpaḥ
ādhāra-śaktim avalambya parāṁ sva-mūrtiṁ
govindam ādi-puruṣaṁ tam ahaṁ bhajāmi

yaḥ—He who; *kāraṇa-arṇava*—of the Causal Ocean; *jale*—in the water; *bhajati*—enjoys; *sma*—indeed; *yoga-nidrām*—creative sleep; *ananta*—unlimited; *jagat-aṇḍa*—universes; *sa*—with; *roma-kūpaḥ*—the pores of His hair; *ādhāra-śaktim*—the all-accommodating potency; *avalambya*—assuming; *parām*—great; *sva-mūrtim*—own subjective form; *govindam*—Govinda; *ādi-puruṣam*—the original person; *tam*—Him; *aham*—I; *bhajāmi*—worship.

I adore the primeval Lord Govinda who assuming His own great subjective form, who bears the name of Śeṣa, replete with the all-accommodating potency, and reposing in the Causal Ocean with the infinity of the world in the pores of His hair, enjoys creative sleep [yoga-nidrā].

PURPORT

(The subjective nature of Ananta who has the form of the couch of Mahā-Viṣṇu, is described.) Ananta, the same who is the infinite couch on which Mahā-Viṣṇu reposes, is a distinctive appearance of the Divinity bearing the name of Śeṣa, having the subjective nature of the servant of Kṛṣṇa.

TEXT 48

यस्यैकनिश्वसितकालमथावलम्ब्य
जीवन्ति लोमविलजा जगदण्डनाथाः ।
विष्णुर्महान् स इह यस्य कलाविशेषो
गोविन्दमादिपुरुषं तमहं भजामि ॥४८॥

yasyaika-niśvasita-kālam athāvalambya
jīvanti loma-vilajā jagad-aṇḍa-nāthāḥ
viṣṇur mahān sa iha yasya kalā-viśeṣo
govindam ādi-puruṣaṁ tam ahaṁ bhajāmi

yasya—whose; *eka*—one; *niśvasita*—of breath; *kālam*—time; *atha*—thus; *avalambya*—taking shelter of; *jīvanti*—live; *loma-vila-jāḥ*—grown from the hair holes; *jagat-aṇḍa-nāthāḥ*—the masters of the universes (the Brahmās); *viṣṇuḥ mahān*—the Supreme Lord Mahā-Viṣṇu; *saḥ*—that; *iha*—here; *yasya*—whose; *kalā-viśeṣaḥ*—particular plenary portion or expansion; *govindam*—Govinda; *ādi-puruṣam*—the original person; *tam*—Him; *aham*—I; *bhajāmi*—worship.

Brahmā and other lords of the mundane worlds, appearing from the pores of hair of Mahā-Viṣṇu, remain alive as long as the duration of one exhalation of the latter [Mahā-Viṣṇu]. I adore the primeval Lord Govinda of whose subjective personality Mahā-Viṣṇu is the portion of portion.

PURPORT

The supreme majesty of the subjective nature of Viṣṇu is shown here.

TEXT 49

भास्वान् यथाश्मसकलेषु निजेषु तेजः
स्वीयम्कियत्प्रकटयत्यपि तद्वदत्र ।
ब्रह्मा य एष जगदण्डविधानकर्ता
गोविन्दमादिपुरुषं तमहं भजामि ॥४९॥

bhāsvān yathāśma-śakaleṣu nijeṣu tejaḥ
svīyaṁ kiyat prakaṭayaty api tadvad atra

brahmā ya eṣa jagad-aṇḍa-vidhāna-kartā
govindam ādi-puruṣaṁ tam ahaṁ bhajāmi

bhāsvān—the illuminating sun; *yathā*—as; *aśma-śakaleṣu*—in various types of precious stones; *nijeṣu*—his own; *tejaḥ*—brilliance; *svīyam*—his own; *kiyat*—to some extent; *prakaṭayati*—manifests; *api*—also; *tadvat*—similarly; *atra*—here; *brahmā*—Lord Brahmā; *yaḥ*—who; *eṣaḥ*—he; *jagat-aṇḍa-vidhāna-kartā*—the chief of the universe; *govindam*—Govinda; *ādi-puruṣam*—the original person; *tam*—Him; *aham*—I; *bhajāmi*—worship.

I adore the primeval Lord Govinda from whom the separated subjective portion Brahmā receives his power for the regulation of the mundane world, just as the sun manifests some portion of his own light in all the effulgent gems that bear the names of sūryakānta, etc.

PURPORT

Brahmā is two types: in certain *kalpas* when the potency of the Supreme Lord infuses Himself in an eligible *jīva*, the latter acts in the office of Brahmā and creates the universe. In those *kalpas* when no eligible *jīva* is available, after the Brahmā of the previous *kalpa* is liberated, Kṛṣṇa, by the process of allotment of His own potency, creates the Brahmā who has the nature of the *avatāra* (descent) of the Divinity in the active mundane principle (*rajo-guṇa*). By principle Brahmā is superior to ordinary *jīvas* but is not the direct Divinity. The divine nature is present in a greater measure in Śambhu than in Brahmā. The fundamental significance of the above is that the aggregate of fifty attributes, belonging to the *jīva*, are present in a fuller measure in Brahmā who possesses, in a lesser degree, five more attributes which are not found in *jīvas*. But in Śambhu both the fifty attributes of *jīvas* as also the five additional attributes found in Brahmā are present in even greater measure than in Brahmā.

TEXT 50

यत्पादपल्लवयुगं विनिधाय कुम्भ-
द्वन्द्वे प्रणामसमये स गणाधिराजः ।
विघ्नान् विहन्तुमलमस्य जगत्त्रयस्य
गोविन्दमादिपुरुषं तमहं भजामि ॥५०॥

yat-pāda-pallava-yugaṁ vinidhāya kumbha-
dvandve praṇāma-samaye sa gaṇādhirājaḥ
vighnān vihantum alam asya jagat-trayasya
govindam ādi-puruṣaṁ tam ahaṁ bhajāmi

yat—whose; *pāda-pallava*—lotus feet; *yugam*—two; *vinidhāya*—having held; *kumbha-dvandve*—upon the pair of tumuli; *praṇāma-samaye*—at the time of offering obeisances; *saḥ*—he; *gaṇa-adhirājaḥ*—Gaṇeśa; *vighnān*—obstacles; *vihantum*—to destroy; *alam*—capable; *asya*—of these; *jagat-trayasya*—three worlds; *govindam*—Govinda; *ādi-puruṣam*—the original person; *tam*—Him; *aham*—I; *bhajāmi*—worship.

I adore the primeval Lord Govinda, whose lotus feet are always held by Gaṇeśa upon the pair of tumuli protruding from his elephant head in order to obtain power for his function of destroying all the obstacles on the path of progress of the three worlds.

PURPORT

The power of destroying all obstacles to mundane prosperity has been delegated to Gaṇeśa who is the object of worship to those who are eligible to worship him. He has obtained a rank among the five gods as Brahmā possessing mundane quality. The self-same Gaṇeśa is a god in possession of delegated power by infusion of the divine power. All his glory rests entirely on the grace of Govinda.

TEXT 51

अग्निर्मही गगनमम्बु मरुद्दिशश्च
कालस्तथात्ममनसीति जगत्त्रयाणि ।
यस्माद्भवन्ति विभवन्ति विशन्ति यं च
गोविन्दमादिपुरुषं तमहं भजामि ॥५१॥

agnir mahī gaganam ambu marud diśaś ca
kālas tathātma-manasīti jagat-trayāṇi
yasmād bhavanti vibhavanti viśanti yaṁ ca
govindam ādi-puruṣaṁ tam ahaṁ bhajāmi

agniḥ—fire; *mahī*—earth; *gaganam*—ether; *ambu*—water; *marut*—air; *diśaḥ*—directions; *ca*—also; *kālaḥ*—time; *tathā*—as well as; *ātma*—soul; *manasī*—and mind; *iti*—thus; *jagat-trayāṇi*—the three worlds; *yasmāt*—from whom; *bhavanti*—they originate; *vibhavanti*—they exist; *viśanti*—they enter; *yam*—whom; *ca*—also; *govindam*—Govinda; *ādi-puruṣam*—the original person; *tam*—Him; *aham*—I; *bhajāmi*—worship.

The three worlds are composed of the nine elements, viz., fire, earth, ether, water, air, direction, time, soul and mind. I adore the primeval Lord Govinda from whom they originate, in whom they exist and into whom they enter at the time of the universal cataclysm.

PURPORT

There is nothing in the three worlds save the five elements, ten quarters, time, *jīva*-soul, and the mental principle allied with the subtle body consisting of mind, intelligence and ego of conditioned souls. The elevationists (*karmīs*) make their offerings in sacrifice in the fire. Conditioned souls know nothing beyond this perceptible world of nine elements. The *jīva* is the self-same soul whose ecstatic delight the joyless liberationists (*jñānīs*) aspire after. Both the principles that are respectively depicted as *ātmā* and *prakṛti* by the system of Sāṅkhya are included in the above. In other words all the principles that have been enunciated by all the speculative philosophers (*tattva-vādīs*) are included in these nine elements. Śrī Govinda is the source of the appearance, continuance and subsidence of all these principles.

TEXT 52

यच्चक्षुरेष सविता सकलग्रहाणां
राजा समस्तसुरमूर्तिरशेषतेजाः ।
यस्याज्ञया भ्रमति सम्भृतकालचक्रो
गोविन्दमादिपुरुषं तमहं भजामि ॥५२॥

yac-cakṣur eṣa savitā sakala-grahāṇāṁ
rājā samasta-sura-mūrtir aśeṣa-tejāḥ
yasyājñayā bhramati sambhṛta-kāla-cakro
govindam ādi-puruṣaṁ tam ahaṁ bhajāmi

yat—of whom; *cakṣuḥ*—the eye; *eṣaḥ*—the; *savitā*—sun; *sakala-grahāṇām*—of all the planets; *rājā*—the king; *samasta-sura*—of all the demigods; *mūrtiḥ*—the image; *aśeṣa-tejāḥ*—full of infinite effulgence; *yasya*—of whom; *ājñayā*—by the order; *bhramati*—performs his journey; *sambhṛta*—complete; *kāla-cakraḥ*—the wheel of time; *govindam*—Govinda; *ādi-puruṣam*—the original person; *tam*—Him; *aham*—I; *bhajāmi*—worship.

The sun who is the king of all the planets, full of infinite effulgence, the image of the good soul, is as the eye of this world. I adore the primeval Lord Govinda in pursuance of whose order the sun performs his journey mounting the wheel of time.

PURPORT

Certain professors of the Vedic religion worship the sun as Brahman. The sun is one of the hierarchy of the five gods. Some people target in heat the source of this world and therefore designate the sun, the only location of heat, as the root cause of this world. Notwithstanding all that may be said to the contrary, the sun is after all only the presiding deity of a sphere of the sum total of all mundane heat and is hence a god exercising delegated authority. The sun performs his specific function of service certainly by the command of Govinda.

TEXT 53

धर्मोऽथ पापनिचयः श्रुतयस्तपांसि
ब्रह्मादिकीटपतगावधयश्च जीवाः ।
यद्दत्तमात्रविभवप्रकटप्रभावा
गोविन्दमादिपुरुषं तमहं भजामि ॥५३॥

dharmo 'tha pāpa-nicayaḥ śrutayas tapāṁsi
brahmādi-kīṭa-patagāvadhayaś ca jīvāḥ
yad-datta-mātra-vibhava-prakaṭa-prabhāvā
govindam ādi-puruṣaṁ tam ahaṁ bhajāmi

dharmaḥ—virtue; *atha*—also; *pāpa-nicayaḥ*—all vices; *śrutayaḥ*—the *Vedas; tapāṁsi*—penances; *brahma-ādi*—beginning from Lord Brahmā; *kīṭa-pataga*—insects; *avadhayaḥ*—down to; *ca*—and; *jīvāḥ*—*jīvas; yat*—by whom; *datta*—conferred; *mātra*—exclusively; *vibhava*—by the power; *prakaṭa*—manifested; *prabhāvāḥ*—potencies; *govindam*—Govinda; *ādi-puruṣam*—the original person; *tam*—Him; *aham*—I; *bhajāmi*—worship.

I adore the primeval Lord Govinda, by whose conferred power are maintained the manifested potencies, that are found to

exist, of all virtues, all vices, the Vedas, the penances and all jīvas, from Brahmā to the meanest insect.

PURPORT

By *dharma* is meant the allotted functions of *varṇa* and *āśrama* manifested by the twenty *dharma-śāstras* on the authority of the *Vedas*. Of these two divisions *varṇa-dharma* is that function which is the outcome of the distinctive natures of the four *varṇas*, viz., *brāhmaṇa*, *kṣatriya*, *vaiśya* and *śūdra* and *āśrama-dharma* is that function which is appropriate to the respective *āśramas* or stations of those who belong to the four stages, viz., *brahmacarya*, *gṛhastha*, *vānaprastha* and *sannyāsa*. All customary activities of mankind have been targeted in these twofold divisions. Sins mean nescience, the root of all sins and sinful desire, also the greatest iniquities and sins flowing from them and the ordinary sins, i.e., all sorts of unprincipled conduct. The category of the *śrutis* means *Ṛg*, *Sāma*, *Yajur* and *Atharva* and the *Upaniṣads* which form the crest jewels of the *Veda*. The *tapas* mean all regular practices that are learnt with the view of the attainment of the proper function of the self. In many cases, e.g., in the form known as *pañca-tapas* these practices are of a difficult character (*yoga*) with its eight constituents limbs and devotedness to the knowledge of the undifferentiated Brahman are included therein. All these are so many distinctive features within the revolving round of the fruitive activities of conditioned souls. The conditioned souls are embarked on a sojourn of successive births from 84 lakhs of varieties of generating organs. They are differentiated into different orders of beings as *devas*, *dānavas*, *rākṣasas*, *mānavas*, *nāgas*, *kinnaras*, and *gandharvas*. These *jīvas*, from Brahmā down to the small insect, are infinite in type. They make up the aggregate of the conditioned souls from the degree of Brahmā to that of the little fly and are the distinctive features within the revolving wheel of *karma*. Every one of them is endowed with distinctive powers as individuals and is powerful in a particular sphere. But these powers are by their nature not fully developed in them. The degree of power and nature of property vary according to the measure of manifestation of the possessions of the individual conferred upon him by Śrī Govinda.

TEXT 54

यस्त्विन्द्रगोपमथवेन्द्रमहो स्वकर्म-
बन्धानुरूपफलभाजनमातनोति ।
कर्माणि निर्दहति किन्तु च भक्तिभाजां
गोविन्दमादिपुरुषं तमहं भजामि ॥५४॥

yas tv indragopam athavendram aho sva-karma-
bandhānurūpa-phala-bhājanam ātanoti
karmāṇi nirdahati kintu ca bhakti-bhājāṁ
govindam ādi-puruṣaṁ tam ahaṁ bhajāmi

yaḥ—He who (Govinda); *tu*—but; *indra-gopam*—to the small red insect called *indragopa; atha vā*—or even; *indram*—to Indra, king of heaven; *aho*—oh; *sva-karma*—of one's own fruitive activities; *bandha*—bondage; *anurūpa*—according to; *phala*—of reactions; *bhājanam*—enjoying or suffering; *ātanoti*—bestows; *karmāṇi*—all fruitive activities and their reactions; *nirdahati*—destroys; *kintu*—but; *ca*—also; *bhakti-bhājām*—of persons engaged in devotional service; *govindam*—Govinda; *ādi-puruṣam*—the original person; *tam*—Him; *aham*—I; *bhajāmi*—worship.

I adore the primeval Lord Govinda, who burns up to their roots all fruitive activities of those who are imbued with devotion and impartially ordains for each the due enjoyment of the fruits of one's activities, of all those who walk in the path of work, in

accordance with the chain of their previously performed works, no less in the case of the tiny insect that bears the name of indragopa than in that of Indra, king of the devas.

PURPORT

God impartially induces the fallen souls to act in the way that is consequent on the deeds of their previous births and to enjoy the fruition of their labors but, out of His great mercy to His devotees, He purges out, by the fire of ordeal, the root of all *karma*, viz., nescience and evil desires. *Karma*, though without beginning, is still perishable. The *karma* of those, who work with the hope of enjoying the fruits of their labors, becomes everlasting and endless and is never destroyed. The function of *sannyāsa* is also a sort of *karma* befitting an *āśrama* and is not pleasant to Kṛṣṇa when it aims at liberation, i.e., desire for emancipation. They also receive fruition of their *karma* and, even if it be disinterested, their *karma* ends in *ātma-mamatā*, i.e., self-pleasure; but those who are pure devotees always serve Kṛṣṇa by gratifying His senses forsaking all attempts of *karma* and *jñāna*, and being free from all desires save that of serving Kṛṣṇa. Kṛṣṇa has fully destroyed the *karma*, its desires and nescience of those devotees. It is a great wonder that Kṛṣṇa, being impartial, is fully partial to His devotees.

TEXT 55

यं क्रोधकामसहजप्रणयादिभीति-
वात्सल्यमोहगुरुगौरवसेव्यभावैः ।
सञ्चिन्त्य तस्य सदृशीं तनुमापुरेते
गोविन्दमादिपुरुषं तमहं भजामि ॥५५॥

yaṁ krodha-kāma-sahaja-praṇayādi-bhīti-
vātsalya-moha-guru-gaurava-sevya-bhāvaiḥ

sañcintya tasya sadṛśīṁ tanum āpur ete
govindam ādi-puruṣaṁ tam ahaṁ bhajāmi

yam—upon whom; *krodha*—wrath; *kāma*—amorous passion; *sahaja-praṇaya*—natural friendly love; *ādi*—and so on; *bhīti*—fear; *vātsalya*—parental affection; *moha*—delusion; *guru-gaurava*—reverence; *sevya-bhāvaiḥ*—and with the attitude of willing service; *sañcintya*—meditating; *tasya*—of that; *sadṛśīm*—befitting; *tanum*—bodily form; *āpuḥ*—attained; *ete*—these persons; *govindam*—Govinda; *ādi-puruṣam*—the original person; *tam*— Him; *aham*—I; *bhajāmi*—worship.

I adore the primeval Lord Govinda, the meditators of whom, by meditating upon Him under the sway of wrath, amorous passion, natural friendly love, fear, parental affection, delusion, reverence and willing service, attain to bodily forms befitting the nature of their contemplation.

PURPORT

Devotion is of two kinds, viz., (1) of the nature of deference to regulation and (2) constituted of natural feeling. *Bhakti* is roused by following with a tinge of faith in the rule of the *śāstras* and instruction of the preceptors. Such *bhakti* is of the nature of loyalty to the scriptural regulations. It continues to be operative as long as the corresponding natural feeling is not roused. If a person loves Kṛṣṇa out of natural tendency, there is the principle of *rāga*, which is no other than a strong desire to serve, which turns into *bhāva* or substantive feeling. When the substantive feeling is aroused the devotee becomes an object of mercy of Kṛṣṇa. It takes much time to attain this stage. Devotion which is of the nature of feeling is superior to that connected with scriptural regulation, soon attains to the realized state and is attractive to Kṛṣṇa. Its various aspects are described in this *śloka*. *Śānta-bhāva*, full of reverence to superior, *dāsya-bhāva*, full of service for carrying out the commands of the object of worship, *sakhya-bhāva* or natural friendly love, *vātsalya-bhāva* or parental affection and *madhura-bhāva* or amorous love, are all included in the category of devotion of the nature of instinctive attachment. But anger, fear and delusion, though they are of the nature of instinctive impulse, are not devotion in the strict sense of the term, because they are not friendly but hostile to the object. Anger is found in *asuras* like Śiśupāla, fear in Kaṁsa, and delusion in the *paṇḍitas* of the pantheistic school. They have the feelings of anger, fear and instinctive impulse marked by complete self-forgetful identification with the nondifferentiated Brahman. But as there is no friendly feeling towards the object of devotion there is no *bhakti*. Again among the feelings of *śānta*, *dāsya*, *sakhya*, *vātsalya* and *madhura—śānta*, though indifferent and dormant in *rāga*, is still reckoned as *bhakti* on account of its being a little friendly. There is an immense volume of *rāga* in the other four varieties of emotion. By the promise of *Gītā*, *ye yathā māṁ prapadyante tāṁs tathaiva bhajāmy aham* ("I serve one according to his submission"), those, who allow themselves to be actuated by the sentiments of fear, anger and delusion, attain to *sāyujya-mukti* (merging in the Absolute). The *śāntas* obtain bodily forms with aptitude for addiction to Brahman and Paramātmā. The *dāsya* and *sakhya* classes of worshipers attain bodily forms characterized by masculine or feminine disposition according to their respective grades of eligibility. The *vātsalya* class of worshipers get bodily forms befitting fatherly and motherly sentiments. The amorous lovers of Kṛṣṇa attain the pure forms of *gopīs* (spiritual milkmaids of Vraja).

TEXT 56

श्रियः कान्ताः कान्तः परमपुरुषः कल्पतरवो
द्रुमा भूमिश्चिन्तामणिगणमयी तोयममृतम् ।

कथा गानं नाट्यं गमनमपि वंशी प्रियसखी
चिदानन्दं ज्योतिः परमपि तदास्वाद्यमपि च ॥
स यत्र क्षीराब्धिः स्रवति सुरभीभ्यश्च सुमहान्
निमेषार्धाख्यो वा व्रजति न हि यत्रापि समयः ।
भजे श्वेतद्वीपं तमहमिह गोलोकमिति यं
विदन्तस्ते सन्तः क्षितिविरलचाराः कतिपये ॥५६॥

śriyaḥ kāntāḥ kāntaḥ parama-puruṣaḥ kalpa-taravo
drumā bhūmiś cintāmaṇi-gaṇa-mayī toyam amṛtam
kathā gānaṁ nāṭyaṁ gamanam api vaṁśī priya-sakhī
cid-ānandaṁ jyotiḥ param api tad āsvādyam api ca

sa yatra kṣīrābdhiḥ sravati surabhībhyaś ca su-mahān
nimeṣārdhākhyo vā vrajati na hi yatrāpi samayaḥ
bhaje śvetadvīpaṁ tam aham iha golokam iti yaṁ
vidantas te santaḥ kṣiti-virala-cārāḥ katipaye

śriyaḥ—Lakṣmīs, goddesses of fortune; *kāntāḥ*—loving consorts; *kāntaḥ*—the enjoyer, lover; *parama-puruṣaḥ*—the Supreme Personality of Godhead; *kalpa-taravaḥ*—desire trees; *drumāḥ*—all the trees; *bhūmiḥ*—the land; *cintāmaṇi-gaṇa-mayī*—made of the transcendental touchstone jewels; *toyam*—the water; *amṛtam*—nectar; *kathā*—talking; *gānam*—song; *nāṭyam*—dancing; *gamanam*—walking; *api*—also; *vaṁśī*—the flute; *priya-sakhī*—constant companion; *cit-ānandam*—transcendental bliss; *jyotiḥ*—effulgence; *param*—the supreme; *api*—also; *tat*—that; *āsvādyam*—everywhere perceived; *api ca*—also; *saḥ*—that; *yatra*—where; *kṣīra-abdhiḥ*—ocean of milk; *sravati*—flows; *surabhībhyaḥ*—from *surabhi* cows; *ca*—and; *su-mahān*—very great; *nimeṣa-ardha*—half a moment; *ākhyaḥ*—called; *vā*—or; *vrajati*—passes away; *na*—not; *hi*—certainly; *yatra*—where; *api*—even; *samayaḥ*—time; *bhaje*—I worship; *śveta-dvīpam*—

Śvetadvīpa; *tam*—that; *aham*—I; *iha*—here; *golokam*—Goloka; *iti*—thus; *yam*—which; *vidantaḥ*—know; *te*—they; *santaḥ*—self-realized souls; *kṣiti*—in this world; *virala*—seldom; *cārāḥ*—going; *katipaye*—few.

I worship that transcendental seat, known as Śvetadvīpa where as loving consorts the Lakṣmīs in their unalloyed spiritual essence practice the amorous service of the Supreme Lord Kṛṣṇa as their only lover; where every tree is a transcendental purpose tree; where the soil is the purpose gem, all water is nectar, every word is a song, every gait is a dance, the flute is the favorite attendant, effulgence is full of transcendental bliss and the supreme spiritual entities are all enjoyable and tasty, where numberless milk cows always emit transcendental oceans of milk; where there is eternal existence of transcendental time, who is ever present and without past or future and hence is not subject to the quality of passing away even for the space of half a moment. That realm is known as Goloka only to a very few self-realized souls in this world.

PURPORT

That region which *jīvas* attain by the best performance of their *rasa-bhajana*, though purely transcendental, is by no means devoid of variegatedness. The nondifferentiated region is attained by indulging in anger, fear and delusion. The devotees attain Goloka, the transcendental region above Vaikuṇṭha, according to the quality of *rasa* of the respective services. In reality that region is no other than Śvetadvīpa or "the White Island," being exceedingly pure. Those, who attain the highest *rasa* in the shape of the realization of pure devotion in this world, viewing the reality of Śvetadvīpa in Gokula, Vṛndāvana and Navadvīpa within this mundane world, designate the same as "Goloka." In that transcendental region of Goloka there are always visible, in their supreme beauty, all the distinctive entities that are incorporated in the pure cognitive principle, viz., the lover and His beloved ones, trees and creepers, mountains, rivers and forests, water, speech, movement, music of the flute, the sun and the moon, tasted and taste (i.e., the unthinkable wonders of the 64 aesthetic arts), milk cows yielding nectarean flow of milk and transcendental ever-existing time.

Descriptions that supply the clue to Goloka are found in various places in the *Vedas* and the other *śāstras* such as the *Purāṇas*, *tantras* etc. The *Chāndogya* says: *brūyād yāvan vā ayam ākāśas tāvan eṣa antar hṛda ākāśaḥ ubhe asmin dyāvā-pṛthivī antar eva samāhite. ubhāv agniś ca vāyuś ca sūrya-candramasāv ubhau vidyun nakṣatrāṇi yac cāsyehāsti yac ca nāsti sarvaṁ tad asmin samāhitam iti.*

The sum and substance of it is that all the variegatedness of this mundane world and much more variety over and above the mundane, are to be found in Goloka. The variety in the transcendental world is fully centralized whereas in the mundane world it is not so and hence productive of weal and woe. The centralized variety of Goloka is unalloyed and full of transcendental cognitive joy. The *Vedas* and *sādhus* practicing devotion revealed by the *Vedas*, by availing the support of their individual cognitional aptitude actuated by devotion, may have a sight of divine realm and by the power of the grace of Kṛṣṇa their tiny cognitive faculty attaining the quality of infinitude they are enabled to be on the level of the plane of enjoyments of Kṛṣṇa.

There is a hidden meaning of the proposition "even the Supreme that is also nevertheless the object of enjoyment" (*param api tad āsvādyam api ca*). The word *param api* indicates that Śrī Kṛṣṇa is the only Truth Absolute in all the transcendental blissful principles and *tad āsvādyam api* means His object of enjoyment. The glory of Rādhā's love for Kṛṣṇa, tasty quality (*rasa*) of Kṛṣṇa that is realized by Rādhā and the bliss of which Rādhā is conscious in the process of such realization, all these threefold *bhāvas* (emotional entities) becoming available for enjoyment by Kṛṣṇa He attains His personality of Śrī Gaurasundara. It is also this that constitutes the transcendental bliss of the delicious loving (*rasa*) service manifested by Śrī Gaurasundara. This also eternally exists only in the selfsame Śvetadvīpa.

TEXT 57

अथोवाच महाविष्णुर्भगवन्तं प्रजापतिम् ।
ब्रह्मन् महत्त्वविज्ञाने प्रजासर्गे च चेन् मतिः ।
पञ्चश्लोकीमिमां विद्यां वत्स दत्तां निबोध मे ॥५७॥

athovāca mahā-viṣṇur
bhagavantaṁ prajāpatim
brahman mahattva-vijñāne
prajā-sarge ca cen matiḥ
pañca-ślokīm imāṁ vidyāṁ
vatsa dattāṁ nibodha me

atha—then; *uvāca*—said; *mahā-viṣṇuḥ*—the Supreme Lord; *bhagavantam*—unto the glorious; *prajāpatim*—Lord Brahmā; *brahman*—O Brahmā; *mahattva*—of the glory (of Godhead); *vijñāne*—in real knowledge; *prajā-sarge*—in creating offspring; *ca*—and; *cet*—if; *matiḥ*—the inclination; *pañca-ślokīm*—five *ślokas*; *imām*—this; *vidyām*—science; *vatsa*—O beloved; *dattām*—given; *nibodha*—hear; *me*—from Me.

On hearing these hymns containing the essence of the truth, the Supreme Lord Kṛṣṇa said to Brahmā, "Brahmā, if you experience the inclination to create offspring by being endowed with the real knowledge of the glory of Godhead, listen, My beloved, from Me to this science set forth in the following five ślokas.

PURPORT

The Supreme Lord became propitious when Brahmā with great eagerness chanted the names, "Kṛṣṇa" and "Govinda" expressive of the form, attribute and pastimes. Brahmā was actuated by the desire for mundane creation. Kṛṣṇa then said to Brahmā how pure unalloyed devotion can be practiced by souls engaged in worldly occupations by combining the same with the desire for carrying out the behest of the Supreme Lord. "The knowledge absolute is knowledge of the glory of Godhead; if you want to procreate offspring being endowed with such knowledge, listen attentively to the science of devotion that is contained in the following five *ślokas*."

(How *bhakti* is practiced by performing worldly duties in the form of carrying out the commands of the Supreme Lord, is being described).

TEXT 58

प्रबुद्धे ज्ञानभक्तिभ्यामात्मन्यानन्दचिन्मयी ।
उदेत्यनुत्तमा भक्तिर्भगवत्प्रेमलक्षणा ॥५८॥

prabuddhe jñāna-bhaktibhyām
ātmany ānanda-cin-mayī
udety anuttamā bhaktir
bhagavat-prema-lakṣaṇā

prabuddhe—when excited; *jñāna*—by cognition or knowledge; *bhaktibhyām*—and by devotional service; *ātmani*—in the pure spirit soul; *ānanda-cit-mayī*—full of knowledge and bliss; *udeti*—is awakened; *anuttamā*—superexcellent; *bhaktiḥ*—devotion; *bhagavat*—for Kṛṣṇa; *prema*—by love; *lakṣaṇā*—characterized.

"When the pure spiritual experience is excited by means of

cognition and service [bhakti], superexcellent unalloyed devotion characterized by love for Godhead is awakened towards Kṛṣṇa, the beloved of all souls.

PURPORT

Real knowledge is nothing but knowledge of one's relationship to the Absolute. Real knowledge is identical with the knowledge of subjective natures of *cit* (animate), *acit* (inanimate) and Kṛṣṇa and of their mutual relationship. Here mental speculation is not alluded to, since that is antagonistic to service (*bhakti*). The knowledge that embraces only the first seven of the ten basic principles (*daśa-mūla*) is the knowledge of relationship. The substantive nature of the spiritual function (*abhidheya*) inculcated by the science of devotion hearing, chanting, meditation, tending His holy feet, worshiping by rituals, making prostrations, doing menial service, practicing friendship and surrendering oneself are identical with practicing the search for Kṛṣṇa. It is specifically described in *Bhakti-rasāmṛta-sindhu.* Devotion (*bhakti*) characterized by love for Godhead makes her appearance by being awakened by such knowledge and practice. Such devotion is superexcellent *bhakti* and is no other than the final object of attainment of all spiritual endeavor of the individual soul (*jīva*).

TEXT 59

प्रमाणैस्तत्सदाचारैस्तदभ्यासैर्निरन्तरम् ।
बोधयन् आत्मनात्मानं भक्तिमप्युत्तमां लभेत् ॥५९॥

pramāṇais tat-sad-ācārais
tad-abhyāsair nirantaram
bodhayan ātmanātmānaṁ
bhaktim apy uttamāṁ labhet

pramāṇaiḥ—by scriptural evidence; *tat*—of them; *sat-ācāraiḥ*—by theistic conduct; *tat*—of them; *abhyāsaiḥ*—by practice; *nirantaram*—constantly; *bodhayan*—awakening; *ātmanā*—by one's own intelligence; *ātmānam*—the self; *bhaktim*—devotion; *api*—certainly; *uttamām*—the highest; *labhet*—one can attain.

"The highest devotion is attained by slow degrees by the method of constant endeavor for self-realization with the help of scriptural evidence, theistic conduct and perseverance in practice.

PURPORT

Evidence—the devotional scriptures, e.g., *Śrīmad-Bhāgavatam*, the *Vedas*, the *Purāṇas*, the *Gītā*, etc. Theistic conduct—the conduct of pious persons (*sādhus*) who are pure devotees and the conduct of those pious persons who practice devotion to Godhead actuated by spontaneous love. Practice—to learn about the ten basic principles (*daśa-mūla*) from the *śāstras* and on receiving the name of Hari as laid down in the same, embodying the name, form, quality and activity of the Divinity, to practice the chanting of the name by serving Him night and day. By this are meant study of the *śāstras* and association with the *sādhus*. The tenfold offense to holy name ceases by serving the name of Hari and simultaneously practicing pious conduct. "Practice" is no other than following the mode of service of the name practiced by the *sādhus* without offense. By perseverance in such practice and devotion characterized by love which is the fruit of spiritual endeavor makes her appearance in the pure essence of the soul.

TEXT 60

यस्याः श्रेयस्करं नास्ति यया निर्वृतिमाप्नुयात् ।
या साधयति मामेव भक्तिं तामेव साधयेत् ॥६०॥

yasyāḥ śreyas-karaṁ nāsti
yayā nirvṛtim āpnuyāt
yā sādhayati mām eva
bhaktiṁ tām eva sādhayet

yasyāḥ—than which; *śreyaḥ-karam*—superior well-being; *na*—not; *asti*—there is; *yayā*—by which; *nirvṛtim*—supreme bliss; *āpnuyāt*—one can attain; *yā*—who; *sādhayati*—leads; *mām*—to Me; eva—certainly; *bhaktim*—loving devotion; *tām*—that; *eva*—indeed; *sādhayet*—one should perform.

"These preliminary practices of devotion [sādhana-bhakti] are conducive to the realization of loving devotion. [Loving devotion]—than whom there is no superior well-being, who goes hand in hand with the attainment of the exclusive state of supreme bliss and who can lead to Myself.

PURPORT

The *jīva*-soul has no better well-being than loving devotion. In this is realized the final beatitude of *jīvas*. The lotus feet of Kṛṣṇa are attainable only by loving devotion. He who cultivates the preliminary devotional activities anxiously keeping in view that realized state of devotion can alone attain to that object of all endeavor. None else can have the same.

TEXT 61

धर्मान् अन्यान् परित्यज्य मामेकं भज विश्वसन् ।
यादृशी यादृशी श्रद्धा सिद्धिर्भवति तादृशी ॥
कुर्वन् निरन्तरं कर्म लोकोऽयमनुवर्तते ।
तेनैव कर्मणा ध्यायन् मां परां भक्तिमिच्छति ॥६१॥

dharmān anyān parityajya
mām ekaṁ bhaja viśvasan

yādṛśī yādṛśī śraddhā
siddhir bhavati tādṛśī

kurvan nirantaraṁ karma
loko 'yam anuvartate
tenaiva karmaṇā dhyāyan
māṁ parāṁ bhaktim icchati

dharmān—meritorious performances; *anyān*—other; *parityajya*—abandoning; *mām*— Me; *ekam*—alone; *bhaja*—serve; *viśvasan*—having faith; *yādṛśī yādṛśī*—just as; *śraddhā*—faith; *siddhiḥ*—realization; *bhavati*—arises; *tādṛśī*—corresponding; *kurvan*—performing; *nirantaram*—ceaselessly; *karma*—activities; *lokaḥ ayam*—the people of this world; *anuvartate*—pursue; *tena*—by those; *eva*—indeed; *karmaṇā*—deeds; *dhyāyan*—meditating; *mām*—upon Me; *parām*—supreme; *bhaktim*—devotion; *icchati*—one obtains.

"Abandoning all meritorious performances serve Me with faith. The realization will correspond to the nature of one's faith. The people of the world act ceaselessly in pursuance of some ideal. By meditating on Me by means of those deeds one will obtain devotion characterized by love in the shape of the supreme service.

PURPORT

The function characterized by unalloyed devotion is the real function of all individual souls (*jīvas*). All other varieties of function are activities of the external cases. These exoteric and esoteric *dharmas* (functions) are manifold, e.g., nondifferential knowledge of the Brahman aiming at extinction of individuality, the *aṣṭāṅga-yoga-dharma* having as its goal attainment of the state of exclusive existence (*kaivalya*), atheistical fruitive ritualism aiming at material enjoyment, *jñāna-yoga-dharma* seeking to combine knowledge with fruitive activity and the practice of the function of barren asceticism. Getting rid of all these, serve Me by pure devotion rooted in faith. Exclusive faith in Me is trust. Faith in the form of trust by the process of gradual purification tends to become a constant engagement (*niṣṭhā*), an object of liking (*ruci*), of attachment (*āsakti*) and a real sentiment (*bhāva*). The more transparent the faith, the greater the degree of realization. If you ask—How will the preservation and conduct of worldly affairs be feasible if one is continuously engaged in the endeavor for the realization of *bhakti*? What also will be the nature of the endeavor for the realization of *bhakti* when the body will perish consequent on the cessation of the function of the body and of society?

In order to strike at the root of this misgiving the Supreme Lord says, "This world subsists by the constant performance of certain activities. Fill all these activities with meditation of Me. This will destroy the quality that makes those activities appear as acts done by you. They will then be of the nature of My service (*bhakti*).

"Mankind live by the threefold activities of body, mind and society. Eating, seating, walking, resting, sleeping, cleansing the body, covering the body, etc., are the various bodily activities; thinking, recollecting, retaining an impression, becoming aware of an entity, feeling pleasure and pain, etc., are the mental feats; marrying, practicing reciprocal relationship between the king and subject, practicing brotherhood, attending at sacrificial meetings, offering oblations, digging wells, tanks, etc., for the benefit of the people, maintaining one's relations, practicing hospitality, observing proper civic conduct, showing due respect to others are the various social activities. When these acts are performed for one's selfish enjoyment, they are called *karma-kāṇḍa;* when the desire for attainment of freedom from activity by knowledge underlies these actions, they are termed *jñāna-yoga* or *karma-yoga*. And when these activities are managed to be performed in this way that is conducive to our endeavor for attainment of *bhakti* they are called *jñāna-bhakta-yoga*, i.e., the subsidiary devotional practices. But only those activities that are characterized by the principle of pure worship are called *bhakti* proper. My meditation is practiced in every act when *bhakti* proper is practiced in due time while performing the subsidiary devotional activities in one's intercourse with the ungodly people of this world. In such position, a *jīva* does not become apathetic to Godhead even by performing those worldly activities. This constitutes the practice of looking inwards, i.e., turning towards one's real self, *vide Īśopaniṣad*—

īśāvāsyam idaṁ sarvaṁ
yat kiñca jagatyāṁ jagat
tena tyaktena bhuñjīthā
mā gṛdhaḥ kasya svid dhanam

The commentator says in regards to this, *tena īśa-tyaktena visṛṣṭena*. The real significance being that if whatever is accepted be received as favor vouchsafed by the Supreme Lord, the worldly activity will cease to be such and will turn into service of Godhead (*bhakti*). So *Īśāvāsya* says *kurvann eveha karmāṇi . . . karma lipyate nare*.

If the worldly acts are performed in the above manner one does not get entangled in *karma* even in hundreds of years of worldly life. The meaning of these two *mantras* from the *jñāna* point of view is renouncement of the fruits of one's worldly actions; but from the *bhakti* point of view they mean the attainment of Kṛṣṇa's favor (*prasādam*) by their transfer to His account. In this method, which is the path of *arcana*, you should do your duties of the world by the meditation of worshiping Godhead thereby. Brahmā cherishes the desire for creation in his heart. If that creative desire is practiced by conjoining the same with the meditation of obeying therein the command of the Supreme Lord, then it will be a subsidiary spiritual function (*gauṇa-dharma*) being helpful for the growth of the disposition for the service of the Divinity by reason of its characteristic of seeking the protection of Godhead. It was certainly proper to instruct Brahmā in this manner. There is no occasion for such instruction in the case of a *jīva* in whom the spontaneous aversion for entities other than Kṛṣṇa manifests itself on his attainment of the substantive entity of spiritual devotion (*bhāva*).

TEXT 62

अहं हि विश्वस्य चराचरस्य
बीजं प्रधानं प्रकृतिः पुमांश्च ।
मयाहितं तेज इदं बिभर्षि
विधे विधेहि त्वमथो जगन्ति ॥६२॥

ahaṁ hi viśvasya carācarasya
bījaṁ pradhānaṁ prakṛtiḥ pumāṁś ca
mayāhitaṁ teja idaṁ bibharṣi
vidhe vidhehi tvam atho jaganti

aham—I; *hi*—certainly; *viśvasya*—of the world; *cara-acarasya*—of animate and inanimate objects; *bījam*—the seed; *pradhānam*—the substance of matter; *prakṛtiḥ*—the material cause; *pumān*—the *puruṣa; ca*—and; *mayā*—by Me; *āhitam*—conferred; *tejaḥ*—fiery energy; *idam*—this; *bibharṣi*—you bear; *vidhe*—O Brahmā; *vidhehi*—regulate; *tvam*—you; *atha u*—now; *jaganti*—the worlds.

"Listen, O Vidhi, I am the seed, i.e., the fundamental principle, of this world of animate and inanimate objects. I am pradhāna [the substance of matter], I am prakṛti [material cause] and I am puruṣa [efficient cause]. This fiery energy that

belongs specially to the Brahman, that inheres in you, has also been conferred by Me. It is by bearing this fiery energy that you regulate this phenomenal world of animate and inanimate objects."

PURPORT

Certain thinkers conclude that the nondifferentiated Brahman is the ultimate entity and by undergoing self-delusion (*vivarta*) exhibits the consciousness of differentiation; or, the limiting principle itself (Māyā), when it is limited, is the phenomenal world and is itself the Brahman, in its unlimited position; or, the Brahman is the substance and this phenomenal world is the reflection; or, everything is an illusion of the *jīva*. Some think that Godhead is evidently a separate entity, *jīva* is another different entity, and the phenomenal world, although it is a singular principle, exists separately as an eternally independent entity; or, Godhead, is the substantive entity and all other entities, as *cit* and *a-cit* attributes, are one in principle. Some suppose that by the force of inconceivable potency sometimes the monistic and sometimes the dualistic principle is realized as the truth. Some again arrive at the conclusion that the theory of the nondual minus all potency is meaningless; whence the Brahman is the one eternally unalloyed entity vested with the pure potency.

These speculations have originated from *Veda* relying on the support of the *Vedānta-sutra*. In these speculations although there is no truth that holds good in all positions, there is yet a certain measure of truth. Not to speak of the anti-Vedic speculations Sāṅkhya, Pātañjala, Nyāya and Vaiśeṣika, nor even of Pūrva-mīmāṁsā which is fond of exclusive fruitive activity in conformity with the teaching of one portion of the *Veda*, the bodies of opinions detailed above have also come into existence by relying outwardly on the *Vedānta* itself. By discarding all these speculations, you and your bona fide community should adopt the ultimate principle identical with the doctrine of *acintya-bhedābheda* (inconceivable simultaneous distinction and nondifference). This will make you eligible for being a true devotee. The basic principle is that this animate world is made up of *jīvas* and the inanimate world is constituted of matter. Of these all the *jīvas* have been manifested by My supreme (*parā*) potency and this phenomenal world has been manifested by My secondary (*aparā*) potency. I am the cause of all causes. In other words, I regulate all of them by the power of My will although I am not a different entity from the marginal and material (*taṭasthā* and *acit*) potencies. By the transformation of those distinct potencies *pradhāna* (substantive material principle), *prakṛti* (material cause) and *puruṣa* (efficient cause) have been produced. Hence although as regards the subjective nature of all potency I am *pradhāna*, *prakṛti* and *puruṣa*, yet as the possessor of power I am eternally distinct from all those potencies. This simultaneous distinction and nondifference has also sprung from My inconceivable power. So let the attainment of love for Kṛṣṇa by the practice of pure devotion through the knowledge of their mutual true relationship that subsists between the *jīva*, the *jaḍa* (matter) and Kṛṣṇa based on the principle of inconceivable simultaneous distinction and non-difference, be My instruction for being handed down in the order of spiritual preceptional succession in your community (Śrī Brahma-sampradāya).

The Author

Śrīla Bhaktisiddhānta Sarasvatī was born in the holy pilgrimage place of Jagannātha Puri to Śrīla Bhaktivinoda Ṭhākura, a great Kṛṣṇa conscious spiritual master in the line of succession coming from Lord Caitanya. Although employed as a government magistrate, Śrīla Bhaktivinoda worked tirelessly to establish the teachings of Lord Caitanya in India, where, unfortunately, the people had come to neglect the principles of devitional service to the Supreme Lord, Kṛṣṇa. He envisioned a worldwide Kṛṣṇa consciousness movement and prayed to the Lord for a son to help him achieve his dream.

On February 6, 1874, in the sacred pilgrimage town of Jagannātha Purī, where Śrīla Bhaktivinoda Ṭhākura served as superintendent of the famous Jagannātha temple, Śrīla Bhaktisiddhānta Sarasvatī appeared in this world. He was given the name Bimala Prasada. At the age of seven, Bimala Prasada had memorized the more than seven hundred Sanskrit verses of the *Bhagavad-gītā* and could speak illuminating commentaries upon them. Śrīla Bhaktivinoda Ṭhākura, the author of many important books and other writings on the philosophy of Kṛṣṇa consciousness, trained his son in printing and proofreading.

By the time he was twenty-five years old, Bimala Prasada had acquired an impressive reputation as a scholar of Sanskrit, mathematics, and astronomy. His astronomical treatise, *Surya-siddhānta*, won him the title Siddhānta Sarasvatī in recognition of his immense learning. In 1905, following the advice of his father, Siddhānta Sarasvatī accepted spiritual initiation from

Gaurakiśora dāsa Bābājī. Although Gaurakiśora dāsa Bābājī was renowned as a saintly person and a great devotee of Lord Kṛṣṇa, he was illiterate. Satisfied with the humility and dedication of his highly educated disciple, Śrīla Gaurakiśora gave him his full blessings and requested him to "preach the Absolute Truth and keep aside all other work." Siddhānta Sarasvatī then proved himself a capable assistant in the missionary work of his father.

Upon the death of Śrīla Bhaktivinoda Ṭhākura in 1914, Siddhānta Sarasvatī became editor of his father's journal, *Sajjana-tosani*, and founded the Bhagawat Press for publication of Kṛṣṇa conscious literature. Then in 1918, Siddhānta Sarasvatī accepted the renounced order of spiritual life, assuming the title Śrīla Bhaktisiddhānta Sarasvatī Gosvāmī Mahārāja. For the purpose of propagating Kṛṣṇa consciousness throughout India, he organized the Gaudiya Math, with sixty-four branches throughout the country. The headquarters of his mission, the Caitanya Gaudiya Math, was located in Śrīdhāma Māyāpur, the birthplace of Lord Caitanya. He would later send disciples to Europe for missionary work.

Śrīla Bhaktisiddhānta Sarasvatī adjusted the traditions of Kṛṣṇa consciousness to conform with the technological and social conditions of the twentieth century. He considered the printing press the most effective means of spreading Kṛṣṇa consciousness throughout the world and was himself the author of many important translations, commentaries, and philosophical essays. He was the first spiritual master to allow his renounced preachers (*sannyāsīs*) to wear Western clothes and travel in modern conveyances rather than on foot.

In 1922, an intelligent young college student named Abhay Caran De happened to visit Śrīla Bhaktisiddhānta at the Gaudiya Math center in Calcutta. Śrīla Bhaktisiddhānta immediately advised the young man that he should preach the message of Kṛṣṇa consciousness to the Western world in the English language. Although not able to immediately carry out Śrīla

Bhaktisiddhānta's desire, Abhay became an active supporter of the Gaudiya Math. In 1933, Abhay formally became a disciple of Śrīla Bhaktisiddhānta, who gave him the name Abhay Caranaravinda.

Throughout the 1930s, Śrīla Bhaktisiddhānta expanded and increased his missionary work and succeeded in reestablishing Kṛṣṇa consciousness as the leading force in Indian spiritual life. Anxious that his work continue, he urged his disciples to form a joint Governing Body Commision to manage the Gaudiya Math in his absence. On January 1, 1937, Śrīla Bhaktisiddhānta Sarasvatī passed from this world. Unfortunately, his leading disciples did not heed his instruction to maintain a Governing Body Commision, and as a result the Gaudiya Math as a united preaching missionary organization gradually disintegrated.

Abhay Caranaravinda, however, remained faithful to the vision of Śrīla Bhaktisiddhānta Sarasvatī that Kṛṣṇa consciousness become a worldwide movement and to the order he personally received from him. He accepted the renounced order of life, *sannyāsa*, assuming the title Bhaktivedanta Swami Mahārāja, and in 1965 traveled to the United States to preach Kṛṣṇa consciousness in the English language. Śrīla Bhaktivedanta Swami founded the International Society for Krishna Consciousness and established a Governing Body Commission, which continues to direct the movement since his departure from this world in 1977. Thus, by the sincere efforts of His Divine Grace A.C. Bhaktivedanta Swami Prabhupāda and his followers, the work of Śrīla Bhaktisiddhānta Sarasvatī is continuing throughout the world.

Glossary

Words in SMALL CAPITALS are defined elsewhere in the Glossary.

Ācārya—one who teaches by personal example; a bona fide spiritual master.

Aniruddha—one of the four primary expansions of the Supreme Lord.

Anubhāva—the resultant outward manifestations of a devotee's loving sentiments for Kṛṣṇa.

Arcana—the devotional practice of worshiping the Deity of the Lord.

Aṣṭāṅga-yogī—a practitioner of the eight-step process of meditation, beginning with sitting postures and breath control.

Asuras—demons.

Ātmā—the self, or soul.

Avatāra—an incarnation.

Bhāgavatam, Śrīmad—the PURĀṆA, or history, written by VYĀSADEVA specifically to bring one to pure devotional service to Lord Kṛṣṇa. This eighteen-thousand-verse scripture was spoken by Śukadeva Gosvāmī five thousand years ago.

Bhakti—devotion to the Supreme Lord.

Bhakti-rasāmṛta-sindhu—RŪPA GOSVĀMĪ'S scriptural treatise on devotional service (available in English as *The Nectar of Devotion*).

Bhaktivinoda Ṭhākura (1838–1915)—the "great-grandfather" of the Kṛṣṇa Consciousness Society; the spiritual master of Śrīla Gaurakiśora dāsa Bābājī and father of Śrīla Bhaktisiddhānta Sarasvatī, who was the spiritual master of Śrīla Prabhupāda.

Bhāva-bhakti—ecstatic devotion to Śrī Kṛṣṇa.

Brahmā—the first created living being and secondary creator of the material universe.

Brahmacarya / Brahmacārī—celibate student life, the first spiritual division of life / one in this order.

Brahma-dhāma—the *brahma-jyoti,* the spiritual effulgence emanating from the transcendental body of Lord Kṛṣṇa and illuminating the spiritual world.

Brāhmaṇa—a member of the intelligent, priestly class.

Chāndogya Upaniṣad—one of the 108 UPANIṢADS, Vedic scriptures.

Cit potency—the knowledge potency.

Cupid—the very beautiful and handsome demigod of material love.

Devas—demigods.

Durgā—the personified material energy of the Lord, and the wife of Lord ŚIVA.

Dvārakā—a city off the coast of Gujarat, India, that was a site of Kṛṣṇa's pastimes.

Gaṇeśa—a great demigod devotee of the Lord.

Gaura(candra) / Gaurasundara—Lord Caitanya Mahāprabhu.

Gītā—*Bhagavad-gītā,* the scripture spoken five thousand years ago by Lord Kṛṣṇa Himself.

Gokula—VṚNDĀVANA, the manifestation of Lord Kṛṣṇa's abode on this planet.

Goloka / Goloka Vṛndāvana—the highest spiritual planet, Lord Kṛṣṇa's personal abode in vaikuṇṭha.

Gopāla-tāpanī—a scripture, one of the 108 UPANIṢADS.

Gopī-jana-vallabha—Kṛṣṇa.

Gopīs—Lord Kṛṣṇa's most confidential eternal servitors in feminine form.

Govardhana—a hill connected with Kṛṣṇa's pastimes in VṚNDĀVANA, India.

Gṛhastha—Kṛṣṇa conscious household life, the second spiritual division of life / one in this order.

Guṇa-avatāras—Viṣṇu (the Supreme Lord), BRAHMĀ and ŚIVA (Śambhu), the presiding deities of the three modes of nature, goodness, passion and ignorance respectively.

Hari—the Supreme Lord.

Hari-bhakti-vilāsa—a scriptural work by SANĀTANA GOSVĀMĪ.

Īśopaniṣad—a scripture that is one of the 108 UPANIṢADS.

Jñānī—one who tries to reach the Supreme Absolute by cultivation of empirical, speculative knowledge.

Kālī—the personified material energy of the Lord.

Kalpa—a period of time equal to one day of BRAHMĀ, or 4,320,000,000 years.
Kāma-bīja—*klīṁ,* the "seed" of the Kāma-gāyatrī *mantra.*
Kaṁsa—a demoniac king who was an enemy of Kṛṣṇa.
Karma—material fruitive activity and reactions.
Kṛṣṇa-sandarbha—a scriptural work by Jīvā Gosvāmī that substantiates Kṛṣṇa's position as the original Supreme Personality of Godhead, source of all expansions and incarnations.
Kṣatriya—a member of the administrative and military class.

Lakhs—hundreds of thousands.

Mahāprabhu—Lord Caitanya Mahāprabhu.
Mahā-Saṅkarṣaṇa—the first SAṄKARṢAṆA expansion of the Supreme Lord.
Mahā-Vaikuṇṭha—*See:* VAIKUṆṬHA.
Maheśvara—Lord śiva.
Mahīṣāsura—a demon who assumed the form of a buffalo.
Mañjarīs—assistants to the GOPĪS.
Mantra-sūktas—Vedic hymns.
Mathurā—a district in Uttar Pradesh, India, where VṚNDĀVANA is situated and that is the site of Lord Kṛṣṇa's appearance and pastimes.
Māyāvāda—relating to an impersonal impersonal conception of the Absolute.
Navadvīpa—the birthplace of Lord Caitanya Mahāprabhu, in Nadia, West Bengal, India.
Niyati—Ramādevī, "the regulator."

Pañcarātra—this extant fifth chapter of *Brahma-saṁhitā.*
Pañca-tapas—five kinds of austerities.
Paramahaṁsa—"topmost-swanlike."
Paravyoma—the spiritual sky.
Pradhāna—the substance of matter.
Pradyumna—one of the four primary expansions of the Supreme Lord.
Prajāpati—BRAHMĀ, the first progenitor.
Prāṇāyāma—breath control, as a means of advancement in YOGA.
Purāṇas—the eighteen historical supplements to the VEDAS.
Puruṣa—"efficient cause," the Supreme Lord as the supreme predominator and enjoyer.
Puruṣa-avatāras—expansions of the Supreme Lord for universal creation, maintenance, and destruction.

Rādhā-kuṇḍa—a sacred pond connected with Kṛṣṇa's pastimes in the area of VṚNDĀVANA, India.

Rajas / rājoguṇa—passion / the material mode of passion.

Rāma—Lord Rāmacandra, an incarnation of Kṛṣṇa as a perfect righteous king.

Rasa—the transcendental "taste" of a particular spiritual relationship with the Supreme Lord.

Rasa-bhajana—an exalted stage of devotional worship to the Lord.

Rāsa-pañcādhyāyī—the five chapters of ŚRĪMAD-BHĀGAVATAM that describe Kṛṣṇa's RĀSA dance.

Rudra—Lord śiva.

Rūpa Gosvāmī—one of the Six Gosvāmīs, contemporaries and followers of Lord Caitanya.

Sādhus—saintly persons.

Sampradāya—disciplic succession.

Sanātana Gosvāmī—one of the Six Gosvāmīs, contemporaries and followers of Lord Caitanya.

Saṅkarṣaṇa—one of the four primary expansions of the Supreme Lord.

Sāṅkhya—the philosophy of analytical study of the elements of the material world, culminating in spiritual realization.

Sannyāsa / sannyāsī—renounced life, the fourth spiritual division of life / one in this order.

Śāstra—scriptures.

Sattva / sattva-guṇa—goodness / material mode of goodness.

Sāttvika—a devotee's transcendental symptoms of ecstatic love for Kṛṣṇa.

Śeṣa Nāga—the transcendental form of the Lord as a snake.

Śiva—an incarnation of the Lord as a demigod who is His agent in the material world, particularly as related to the mode of ignorance.

Śloka—a verse, especially of the VEDAS.

Śrī / Śrīla / etc.—See name following title.

Śrīmad-Bhāgavatam—*See:* BHĀGAVATAM, ŚRĪMAD.

Śūdra—a member of the worker or servant class.

Sūktas—Vedic hymns.

Tamas / tamo-guṇa—ignorance / material mode of ignorance.

Tantras-śāstras—a particular division of Vedic scripture.

Ṭhākura Bhaktivinoda—*See:* BHAKTIVINODA ṬHĀKURA.

Ṭhākura Vṛndāvana—*See:* VṚNDĀVANA DĀSA ṬHĀKURA.

Ujjvala-nīlamaṇi—a scriptural work by RŪPA GOSVĀMĪ.
Upaniṣads—108 philosophical treatises that appear within the VEDAS.
Vaikuṇṭha—the eternal spiritual world, "without anxiety," beyond the material cosmos.
Vaiṣṇava—relating to devotional service to Lord Viṣṇu, or Kṛṣṇa; a devotee of Lord Viṣṇu, or Kṛṣṇa.
Vaiśya—a member of the farming and mercantile class.
Vānaprastha—retired life, the third spiritual division of life / one in this order.
Vāsudeva—one of the four primary expansions of the Supreme Lord.
Vedas—the original revealed scriptures, first spoken by the Lord Himself.
Vibhāva—the particular type of ecstatic loving sentiment for Kṛṣṇa that develops in a devotee's heart.
Vraja(bhūmi)—*See:* VṚNDĀVANA.
Vraja-maṇḍala—the area of VṚNDĀVANA, India.
Vṛndāvana—the eternal abode of Lord Kṛṣṇa manifested on this planet in MATHURĀ, India.
Vṛndāvana dāsa Ṭhākura—the author of *Caitanya-bhāgavata,* a scriptural biography of Lord Caitanya Mahāprabhu.
Vyabhicārī—"disturbing" symptoms of a devotee's ecstatic love for Kṛṣṇa.
Vyāsa(deva)—"the literary incarnation of the Lord," compiler and author of Vedic literature.

Yamunā—a sacred river in India that flows through the VṚNDĀVANA area.
Yoga—a spiritual discipline to link oneself with the Supreme.
Yogamāyā—the personified internal, spiritual energy of the Lord.
Yogī—a YOGA practitioner.

Sanskrit Pronunciation Guide

Throughout the centuries, the Sanskrit language has been written in a variety of alphabets. The mode of writing most widely used throughout India, however, is called *devanāgarī,* which means, literally, the writing used in "the cities of the demigods." The *devanāgarī* alphabet consists of forty-eight characters: thirteen vowels and thirty-five consonants. Ancient Sanskrit grammarians arranged this alphabet according to practical linguistic principles, and this order has been accepted by all Western scholars. The system of transliteration used in this book conforms to a system that scholars have accepted to indicate the pronunciation of each Sanskrit sound.

Vowels

अ **a** आ **ā** इ **i** ई **ī** उ **u** ऊ **ū** ऋ **ṛ**

ॠ **ṝ** ऌ **ḷ** ए **e** ऐ **ai** ओ **o** औ **au**

Consonants

Gutturals:	क **ka**	ख **kha**	ग **ga**	घ **gha**	ङ **ṅa**
Palatals:	च **ca**	छ **cha**	ज **ja**	झ **jha**	ञ **ña**
Cerebrals:	ट **ṭa**	ठ **ṭha**	ड **ḍa**	ढ **ḍha**	ण **ṇa**
Dentals:	त **ta**	थ **tha**	द **da**	ध **dha**	न **na**
Labials:	प **pa**	फ **pha**	ब **ba**	भ **bha**	म **ma**
Semivowels:	य **ya**	र **ra**	ल **la**	व **va**	
Sibilants:	श **śa**	ष **ṣa**	स **sa**		
Aspirate:	ह **ha**	Anusvāra: ं **ṁ**		Visarga: ः **ḥ**	

Numerals

० – 0 १ – 1 २ – 2 ३ – 3 ४ – 4 ५ – 5 ६ – 6 ७ – 7 ८ – 8 ९ – 9

The vowels appear as follows in conjunction with a consonant:

ा **ā** ि **i** ी **ī** ु **u** ू **ū** ृ **ṛ** ॄ **ṝ** े **e** ै **ai** ो **o** ौ **au**

For example: क **ka** का **kā** कि **ki** की **kī** कु **ku** कू **kū**
कृ **kṛ** कॄ **kṝ** कॢ **kḷ** के **ke** कै **kai** को **ko**
कौ **kau**

Generally two or more consonants in conjunction are written together in a special form, as for example: क्ष **kṣa** त्र **tra**
The vowel "**a**" is implied after a consonant with no vowel symbol.
The symbol *virāma* (्) indicates that there is no ènal vowel: क्

The vowels are pronounced as follows:

a — as in b**u**t
ā — as in f**a**r but held twice as long as **a**
i — as in p**i**n
ī — as in p**i**que but held twice as long is **i**
u — as in p**u**sh
ū — as in r**u**le but held twice as long as **u**
ṛ — as in **ri**m
ṝ — as in **ree**d but held twice as long as **ṛ**
ḷ — as in happi**ly**
e — as in th**ey**
ai — as in **ai**sle
o — as in g**o**
au — as in h**ow**

The consonants are pronounced as follows:

Gutturals
(pronounced from the throat)

k — as in **k**ite
kh — as in Ec**kh**art
g — as in **g**ive
gh — as in di**g-h**ard
ṅ — as in si**ng**

Palatals
(pronounced with the middle of the tongue against the palate)

c — as in **ch**air
ch — as in staun**ch-h**eart
j — as in **j**oy
jh — as in he**dgeh**og
ñ — as in ca**ny**on

Cerebrals

(pronounced with the tip of the tongue against the roof of the mouth)

ṭ — as in **t**ub

ṭh — as in ligh**t-h**eart

ḍ — as in **d**ove

ḍh — as in re**d-h**ot

ṅ — as in si**ng**

Labials

(pronounced with the lips)

p — as in **p**ine

ph — as in u**p-h**ill (not f)

b — as in **b**ird

bh — as in ru**b-h**ard

m — as in **m**other

Dentals

(pronounced like the cerebrals but with the tongue against the teeth)

t — as in **t**ub

th — as in ligh**t-h**eart

d — as in **d**ove

dh — as in re**d-h**ot

n — as in **n**ut

Semivowels

y — as in **y**es

r — as in **r**un

l — as in **l**ight

v — as in **v**ine, except when preceded in the same syllable by a consonant; then as in s**w**an

Sibilants

ś — as in the German word **s**prechen

ṣ — as in **sh**ine

s — as in **s**un

Aspirate

h — as in **h**ome

Visarga

ḥ — a ènal h-sound: **aḥ** is pronounced like **aha**; **iḥ** like **ihi**.

Anusvara

ṁ — a resonant nasal sound as in the French word *bo***n**

There is no strong accentuation of syllables in Sanskrit, or pausing between words in a line. There is only a Íowing of short and long syllables (the long twice as long as the short). A long syllable is one whose vowel is long (**ā, ī, ū, ṝ, e, ai, o, au**) or whose short vowel is followed by more than one consonant. The letters **ḥ** and **ṁ** count as consonants. Aspirated consonants (consonants followed by an **h**) count as single consonants.

Index of Sanskrit Verses

This index constitutes a complete listing of the first lines of the verses of the *Brahma-saṁhitā,* arranged in English alphabetical order. Numerals refer to verse numbers.

General Index

Numerals indicate text numbers rather than page numbers. Numerals in parenthesis indicate paragraph numbers within the text of the purport. Numerals in boldface type indicate references to translations of verses of the *Brahma-saṁhitā*.

The International Society for Krishna Consciousness
Founder-*Ācārya:* His Divine Grace A.C. Bhaktivedanta Swami Prabhupāda

CENTERS AROUND THE WORLD

CANADA

Brampton-Mississauga, Ontario — Unit 20, 1030 Kamato Dr., L4W 4B6/Tel. (416) 840-6587 or (905) 826-1290/ iskconbrampton@gmail.com
Calgary, Alberta — 313 Fourth St. N.E., T2E 3S3/ Tel. (403) 265-3302/ Fax: (403) 547-0795/vamanstones@shaw.ca
Edmonton, Alberta — 9353 35th Ave. NW, T6E 5R5/ Tel. (780) 439-9999/ harekrishna.edmonton@gmail.com
Montreal, Quebec — 1626 Pie IX Blvd., H1V 2C5/ Tel. & fax: (514) 521-1301/ iskconmontreal@gmail.com
◆ **Ottawa, Ontario** — 212 Somerset St. E., K1N 6V4/ Tel. (613) 565-6544/ Fax: (613) 565-2575/ iskconottawa@sympatico.ca
Regina, Saskatchewan — 1279 Retallack St., S4T 2H8/ Tel. (306) 525-0002 or -6461/jagadishadas@yahoo.com
Toronto, Ontario — 243 Avenue Rd., M5R 2J6/ Tel. (416) 922-5415/ Fax: (416) 922-1021/ toronto@iskcon.net
Vancouver, B.C. — 5462 S.E. Marine Dr., Burnaby V5J 3G8/ Tel. (604) 433-9728/ Fax: (604) 648-8715/akrura@krishna.com; Govinda's Bookstore & Cafe/ Tel. (604) 433-7100 or 1-888-433-8722

RURAL COMMUNITY

Ashcroft, B.C. — Saranagati Dhama, Venables Valley (mail: P.O. Box 99, VOK 1A0)/ Tel. (250) 457-7438/Fax: (250) 453-9306/ iskconsaranagati@hotmail.com

U.S.A.

Atlanta, Georgia — 1287 South Ponce de Leon Ave. N.E., 30306/ Tel. & fax: (404) 377-8680/ admin@atlantaharekrishnas.com
Austin, Texas — 10700 Jonwood Way, 78753/ Tel. (512) 835-2121/ Fax: (512) 835-8479/ sda@backtohome.com
Baltimore, Maryland —200 Bloomsbury Ave., Catonsville, 21228/ Tel. (410) 719-1776/ Fax: (410) 799-0642/ info@baltimorekrishna.com
Berkeley, California — 2334 Stuart St., 94705/ Tel. (510) 649-8619/ Fax: (510) 665-9366/ rajan416@yahoo.com
Boise, Idaho — 1615 Martha St., 83706/ Tel. (208) 344-4274/ boise_temple@yahoo.com
Boston, Massachusetts — 72 Commonwealth Ave., 02116/ Tel. (617) 247-8611/ Fax: (617) 909-5181/ darukrishna@iskconboston.org
Chicago, Illinois — 1716 W. Lunt Ave., 60626/ Tel. (773) 973-0900/ Fax: (773) 973-0526/ chicagoiskcon@yahoo.com
Columbus, Ohio — 379 W. Eighth Ave., 43201/ Tel. (614) 421-1661/ Fax: (614) 294-0545/ rmanjari@sbcglobal.net
◆ **Dallas, Texas** — 5430 Gurley Ave., 75223/ Tel. (214) 827-6330/ Fax: (214) 823-7264/ txkrishnas@aol.com; restaurant: vegetariantaste@aol.com
◆ **Denver, Colorado** — 1400 Cherry St., 80220/ Tel. (303) 333-5461/ Fax: (303) 321-9052/ info@krishnadenver.com
Detroit, Michigan — 383 Lenox Ave., 48215/ Tel. (313) 824-6000/ gaurangi108@hotmail.com
Gainesville, Florida — 214 N.W. 14th St., 32603/ Tel. (352) 336-4183/ Fax: (352) 379-2927/ kalakantha.acbsp@pamho.net
Hartford, Connecticut — 1683 Main St., E. Hartford 06108/ Tel. & fax: (860) 289-7252/ pyari@sbcglobal.net
◆ **Honolulu, Hawaii** — 51 Coelho Way, 96817/ Tel. (808) 595-4913/ rama108@bigfoot.com
Houston, Texas — 1320 W. 34th St., 77018/ Tel. (713) 686-4482/ Fax: (713) 956-9968/ management@iskconhouston.org
Kansas City, Missouri — 5201 Paseo Blvd./ Tel. (816) 924-5619/ Fax: (816) 924-5640/ rvc@rvc.edu
Laguna Beach, California — 285 Legion St., 92651/ Tel. (949) 494-7029/ info@lagunatemple.com
Las Vegas, Nevada — Govinda's Center of Vedic India, 6380 S. Eastern Ave., Suite 8, 89120/ Tel. (702) 434-8332/ info@govindascenter.com
◆ **Los Angeles, California** — 3764 Watseka Ave., 90034/ Tel. (310) 836-2676/ Fax: (310) 839-2715/ membership@harekrishnala.com
◆ **Miami, Florida** — 3220 Virginia St., 33133 (mail: 3109 Grand Ave. #491, Coconut Grove, FL 33133)/ Tel. (305) 442-7218/ devotionalservice@iskcon-miami.org
New Orleans, Louisiana — 2936 Esplanade Ave., 70119/ Tel. (504) 304-0032 (office) or (504) 638-3244/ iskcon.new.orleans@pamho.net
◆ **New York, New York** — 305 Schermerhorn St., Brooklyn 11217/ Tel. (718) 855-6714/ Fax: (718) 875-6127/ ramabhadra@aol.com
New York, New York — 26 Second Ave., 10003/ Tel. (212) 253-6182/ krishnanyc@gmail.com
Orlando, Florida — 2651 Rouse Rd., 32817/ Tel. (407) 257-3865
Philadelphia, Pennsylvania — 41 West Allens Lane, 19119/ Tel. (215) 247-4600/ Fax: (215) 247-8702/ savecows@aol.com
◆ **Philadelphia, Pennsylvania** — 1408 South St., 19146/ Tel. (215) 985-9303/ savecows@aol.com
Phoenix, Arizona — 100 S. Weber Dr., Chandler, 85226/ Tel. (480) 705-4900/ Fax: (480) 705-4901/ svgd108@yahoo.com
Portland, Oregon — 2095 NW Alocleck Dr., Suites 1107 & 1109, Hillsboro 97124/ Tel. (503) 439-9117/ info@iskconportland.com
St. Augustine, Florida — 3001 First St., 32084/ Tel. & fax: (904) 819-0221/ vasudeva108@gmail.com
◆ **St. Louis, Missouri** — 3926 Lindell Blvd., 63108/ Tel. (314) 535-8085 or 534-1708/ Fax: (314) 535-0672/ rpsdas@gmail.com
San Antonio, Texas — 6772 Oxford Trace, 78240/ Tel. (210) 401-6576/ aadasa@gmail.com
◆ **San Diego, California** — 1030 Grand Ave., Pacific

◆ Temples with restaurants or dining

Beach 92109/ Tel. (310) 895-0104/ Fax: (858) 483-0941/ krishna.sandiego@gmail.com
San Jose, California — 951 S. Bascom Ave., 95128/ Tel. (408) 293-4959/ iskconsanjose@yahoo.com
Seattle, Washington — 1420 228th Ave. S.E., Sammamish 98075/ Tel. (425) 246-8436/ Fax: (425) 868-8928/ info@vedicculturalcenter.org
◆ **Spanish Fork, Utah** — Krishna Temple Project & KHQN Radio, 8628 S. State Rd., 84660/ Tel. (801) 798-3559/ Fax: (810) 798-9121/ carudas@earthlink.net
Tallahassee, Florida — 1323 Nylic St., 32304/ Tel. & fax: (850) 224-3803/ darudb@hotmail.com
Towaco, New Jersey — 100 Jacksonville Rd. (mail: P.O. Box 109), 07082/ Tel. & fax: (973) 299-0970/ newjersey@iskcon.net
◆ **Tucson, Arizona** — 711 E. Blacklidge Dr., 85719/ Tel. (520) 792-0630/ Fax: (520) 791-0906/ tucphx@cs.com
Washington, D.C. — 10310 Oaklyn Dr., Potomac, Maryland 20854/ Tel. (301) 299-2100/ Fax: (301) 299-5025/ ad@pamho.net

RURAL COMMUNITIES

◆ **Alachua, Florida (New Raman Reti)** — 17306 N.W. 112th Blvd., 32615 (mail: P.O. Box 819, 32616)/ Tel. (386) 462-2017/ Fax: (386) 462-2641/ alachuatemple@gmail.com
Carriere, Mississippi (New Talavan) — 31492 Anner Road, 39426/ Tel. (601) 749-9460 or 799-1354/ Fax: (601) 799-2924/ talavan@hughes.net
Gurabo, Puerto Rico (New Govardhana Hill) — Carr. 181, Km. 16.3, Bo. Santa Rita, Gurabo (mail: HC-01, Box 8440, Gurabo, PR 00778)/ Tel. (787) 367-3530 or (787) 737-1722/ manonath@gmail.com
Hillsborough, North Carolina (New Goloka) — 1032 Dimmocks Mill Rd., 27278/ Tel. (919) 732-6492/ bkgoswami@earthlink.net
Moundsville, West Virginia (New Vrindaban) — R.D. No. 1, Box 319, Hare Krishna Ridge, 26041/ Tel. (304) 843-1600; Visitors, (304) 845-5905/ Fax: (304) 845-0023/ mail@newvrindaban.com
Mulberry, Tennessee (Murari-sevaka) — 532 Murari Lane, 37359 (mail: P.O. Box 108, Lynchburg, TN 37352)/ Tel. (931) 227-6156/ Tel. & fax: (931) 759-6888/ murari_sevaka@yahoo.com
Port Royal, Pennsylvania (Gita Nagari) — 534 Gita Nagari Rd./ Tel. (717) 527-4101/ kaulinidasi@hotmail.com
Sandy Ridge, North Carolina — Prabhupada Village, 1283 Prabhupada Rd., 27046/ Tel. (336) 593-9888/ madanmohanmohinni@yahoo.com

ADDITIONAL RESTAURANTS

Hato Rey, Puerto Rico — Tamal Krishna's Veggie Garden, 131 Eleanor Roosevelt, 00918/ Tel. (787) 754-6959/ Fax: (787) 756-7769/ tkveggiegarden@aol.com
Seattle, Washington — My Sweet Lord, 5521 University Way, 98105/ Tel. (425) 643-4664

UNITED KINGDOM AND IRELAND

Belfast, Northern Ireland — Brooklands, 140 Upper Dunmurray Lane, BT17 OHE/ Tel. +44 (28) 9062 0530
Birmingham, England — 84 Stanmore Rd., Edgbaston B16 9TB/ Tel. +44 (121) 420 4999/ birmingham@iskcon.org.uk
Cardiff, Wales — The Soul Centre, 116 Cowbridge Rd., East Canton CF11 9DX/ Tel. +44 (29) 2039 0391/ the.soul.centre@pamho.net
Coventry, England — Kingfield Rd., Coventry (mail: 19 Gloucester St., Coventry CV1 3BZ)/ Tel. +44 (24) 7655 2822 or 5420/ haridas.kds@pamho.net
◆ **Dublin, Ireland** — 83 Middle Abbey St., Dublin 1/ Tel. +353 (1) 661 5095/ dublin@krishna.ie; Govinda's: info@govindas.ie
Lesmahagow, Scotland — Karuna Bhavan, Bankhouse Rd., Lesmahagow, Lanarkshire, ML11 0ES/ Tel. +44 (1555) 894790/ Fax: +44 (1555) 894526/ karunabhavan@aol.com
Leicester, England — 21 Thoresby St., North Evington, LE5 4GU/ Tel. +44 (116) 276 2587/ pradyumna.jas@pamho.net
◆ **London, England (city)** — 10 Soho St., W1D 3DL/ Tel. +44 (20) 7437-3662; residential /pujaris, 7439-3606; shop, 7287-0269; Govinda's Restaurant, 7437-4928/ Fax: +44 (20) 7439-1127/ london@pamho.net
◆ **London, England (country)** — Bhaktivedanta Manor, Dharam Marg, Hilfield Lane, Watford, Herts, WD25 8EZ/ Tel. +44 (1923) 851000/ Fax: +44 (1923) 851006/ info@krishnatemple.com; Guesthouse: bmguesthouse@krishna.com
London, England (south) — 42 Enmore Road, South Norwood, SE25 5NG/ Tel. +44 7988857530/ krishnaprema89@hotmail.com
London, England (Kings Cross) — 102 Caledonain Rd., Kings Cross, Islington, N1 9DN/ Tel. +44 (20) 7168 5732/ foodforalluk@aol.com
Manchester, England — 20 Mayfield Rd., Whalley Range, M16 8FT/ Tel. +44 (161) 226 4416/ contact@iskconmanchester.com
Newcastle-upon-Tyne, England — 304 Westgate Rd., NE4 6AR/ Tel. +44 (191) 272 1911
◆ **Swansea, Wales** — 8 Craddock St., SA1 3EN/ Tel. +44 (1792) 468469/ iskcon.swansea@pamho.net (restaurant: govindas@hotmail.com)

RURAL COMMUNITIES

Upper Lough Erne, Northern Ireland — Govindadwipa Dhama, Inisrath Island, Derrylin, Co. Fermanagh, BT92 9GN/ Tel. +44 (28) 6772 1512/ govindadwipa@pamho.net
London, England — (contact Bhaktivedanta Manor) Programs are held regularly in more than forty other cities in the UK. For information, contact ISKCON Reader Services, P.O. Box 730, Watford WD25 8EZ, UK; www.iskcon.org.uk

ADDITIONAL RESTAURANTS

Dublin, Ireland — Govinda's, 4 Aungier St., Dublin 2/ Tel. +353 (1) 475 0309/ Fax: +353 (1) 478 6204/ info@govindas.ie
Dublin, Ireland — Govinda's, 18 Merrion Row, Dublin 2/ Tel. +353 (1) 661 5095/ praghosa.sdg@pamho.net

AUSTRALASIA

AUSTRALIA

Adelaide — 25 Le Hunte St. (mail: P.O. Box 114, Kilburn, SA 5084)/ Tel. & fax: +61 (8) 8359-5120/ iskconsa@tpg.com.au
Brisbane — 95 Bank Rd., Graceville (mail: P.O. Box 83, Indooroopilly), QLD 4068/ Tel. +61 (7) 3379-5455/ Fax: +61 (7) 3379-5880/ brisbane@iskcon.org.au
Canberra — 1 Quick St., Ainslie, ACT 2602 (mail: P.O. Box 1411, Canberra, ACT 2601)/ Tel. & fax: +61 (2) 6262-6208/ iskcon@harekrishnacanberra.com
Melbourne — 197 Danks St. (mail: P.O. Box 125), Albert Park, VIC 3206/ Tel. +61 (3) 9699-5122/ Fax: +61 (3) 9690-4093/ melbourne@pamho.net
Newcastle — 28 Bull St., Mayfield, NSW 2304/ Tel. +61 (2) 4967-7000/ iskcon_newcastle@yahoo.com.au
Perth — 155–159 Canning Rd., Kalamunda (mail: P.O. Box 201 Kalamunda 6076)/ Tel. +61 (8) 6293-1519/ perth@pamho.net
Sydney — 180 Falcon St., North Sydney, NSW 2060 (mail: P.O. Box 459, Cammeray, NSW 2062)/ Tel. +61 (2) 9959-4558/ Fax: +61 (2) 9957-1893/ admin@iskcon.com.au
Sydney — Govinda's Yoga & Meditation Centre, 112 Darlinghurst Rd., Darlinghurst NSW 2010 (mail: P.O. Box 174, Kings Cross 1340)/ Tel. +61 (2) 9380-5162/ Fax: +61 (2) 9360-1736/ sita@govindas.com.au

RURAL COMMUNITIES

Bambra, VIC (New Nandagram) — 50 Seaches Outlet, off 1265 Winchelsea Deans Marsh Rd., Bambra VIC 3241/ Tel. +61 (3) 5288-7383
Cessnock, NSW (New Gokula) — Lewis Lane (Off Mount View Road, Millfield, near Cessnock [mail: P.O. Box 399, Cessnock, NSW 2325])/ Tel. +61 (2) 4998-1800/ Fax: (Sydney temple)/ iskconfarm@mac.com
Murwillumbah, NSW (New Govardhana) — Tyalgum Rd., Eungella (mail: P.O. Box 687), NSW 2484/ Tel. +61 (2) 6672-6579/ Fax: +61 (2) 6672-5498/ ajita@in.com.au

RESTAURANTS

Brisbane — Govinda's, 99 Elizabeth St., 1st Floor, QLD 4000/ Tel. +61 (7) 3210-0255
Brisbane — Krishna's Cafe, 1st Floor, 82 Vulture St., W. End, QLD 4000/ brisbane@pamho.net
Burleigh Heads — Govindas, 20 James St., Burleigh Heads, QLD 4220/ Tel. +61 (7) 5607-0782/ ajita@in.com.au
Cairns — Gaura Nitai's, 55 Spence St., Cairns, QLD/ Tel. +61 (7) 4031-2255 or (425) 725 901/ Fax: +61 (7) 4031 2256/ gauranitais@in.com.au
Maroochydore — Govinda's Vegetarian Cafe, 2/7 First Ave., QLD 4558/ Tel. +61 (7) 5451-0299
Melbourne — Crossways, 1st Floor, 123 Swanston St., VIC 3000/ Tel. +61 (3) 9650-2939
Melbourne — Gopal's, 139 Swanston St., VIC 3000/ Tel. +61 (3) 9650-1578
Newcastle — Govinda's Vegetarian Cafe, 110 King St., corner of King & Wolf Streets, NSW 2300/ Tel. +61 (2) 4929-6900 / info@govindascafe.com.au
Perth — Hare Krishna Food for Life, 200 William St., Northbridge, WA 6003/ Tel. +61 (8) 9227-1684/ iskconperth@optusnet.com.au

NEW ZEALAND AND FIJI

Auckland, NZ — The Loft, 1st Floor, 103 Beach Rd./ Tel. +64 (9) 3797301
Christchurch, NZ — 83 Bealey Ave. (mail: P.O. Box 25-190)/ Tel. +64 (3) 366-5174/ Fax: +64 (3) 366-1965/ iskconchch@clear.net.nz
Hamilton, NZ — 188 Maui St., RD 8, Te Rapa/ Tel. +64 (7) 850-5108/ rmaster@wave.co.nz
Labasa, Fiji — Delailabasa (mail: P.O. Box 133)/ Tel. +679 812912
Lautoka, Fiji — 5 Tavewa Ave. (mail: P.O. Box 125)/ Tel. +679 666 4112/ regprakash@excite.com
Nausori, Fiji — Hare Krishna Cultural Centre, 2nd Floor, Shop & Save Building 11 Gulam Nadi St., Nausori Town (mail: P.O. Box 2183, Govt. Bldgs., Suva)/ Tel. +679 9969748 or 3475097/ Fax: +679 3477436/ vdas@frca.org.fj
Rakiraki, Fiji — Rewasa (mail: P.O. Box 204)/ Tel. +679 694243
Sigatoka, Fiji — Queens Rd., Olosara (mail: P.O. Box 1020)/ Tel. +679 6520866 or 6500349/ drgsmarna@connect.com.fj
Suva, Fiji — 166 Brewster St. (mail: P.O. Box 4229, Samabula)/ Tel. +679 331 8441/ Fax: +679 3100016/ iskconsuva@connect.com.fj
Wellington, NZ — 105 Newlands Rd., Newlands/ Tel. +64 (4) 478-4108/ info@iskconwellington.org.nz
Wellington, NZ — Gaura Yoga Centre, 1st Floor, 175 Vivian St. (mail: P.O. Box 6271, Marion Square)/ Tel. +64 (4) 801-5500/ yoga@gaurayoga.co.nz

RURAL COMMUNITY

Auckland, NZ (New Varshan) — Hwy. 28, Riverhead, next to Huapai Golf Course (mail: R.D. 2, Kumeu)/ Tel. +64 (9) 412-8075/ Fax: +64 (9) 412-7130

RESTAURANTS

Auckland, NZ — Hare Krishna Food for Life, 268 Karangahape Rd./ Tel. +64 (9) 300-7585
Labasa, Fiji — Hare Krishna Restaurant, Naseakula Road/ Tel. +679 811364
Lautoka, Fiji — Gopal's, Corner of Yasawa Street and Naviti Street/ Tel. +679 662990
Suva, Fiji — Hare Krishna Vegetarian Restaurant, Dolphins FNPF Place, Victoria Parade/ Tel. +679 314154/ vdas@govnet.gov.fj
Suva, Fiji — Hare Krishna Vegetarian Restaurant, Opposite University of the South Pacific, Laucala Bay Rd./ Tel. +679 311683/ vdas@govnet.gov.fj
Suva, Fiji — Hare Krishna Vegetarian Restaurant, 18 Pratt St./ Tel. +679 314154
Suva, Fiji — Hare Krishna Vegetarian Restaurant, 82 Ratu Mara Rd., Samabula/ Tel. +679 386333
Suva, Fiji — Hare Krishna Vegetarian Restaurant, Terry Walk, Cumming St./ Tel. +679 312295
Wellington, NZ — Higher Taste Hare Krishna Restaurant, Old Bank Arcade, Ground Flr., Corner Customhouse, Quay & Hunter St., Wellington/ Tel. +64 (4) 472-2233/ Fax: (4) 472-2234/ highertaste@iskconwellington.orgorg.nz

INDIA (partial list)*

Ahmedabad, Gujarat — Satellite Rd., Gandhinagar Highway Crossing, 380 054/ Tel. (079) 686-1945, -1645, or -2350/ jasomatinandan.acbsp@pamho.net

Allahabad, UP — Hare Krishna Dham, 161 Kashi Raj Nagar, Baluaghat 211 003/ Tel. (0532) 415294

Amritsar, Punjab — Chowk Moni Bazar, Laxmansar, 143 001/ Tel. (0183) 2540177

Bangalore, Karnataka — Hare Krishna Hill, Chord Rd., 560 010/ Tel. (080) 23471956 or 23578346/ Fax: (080) 23578625/ manjunath36@iskconbangalore.org

Bangalore, Karnataka — ISKCON Sri Jagannath Mandir, No.5 Sripuram, 1st cross, Sheshadripuram, Bangalore 560 020/ Tel. (080) 3536867 or 2262024 or 3530102

Baroda, Gujarat — Hare Krishna Land, Gotri Rd., 390 021/ Tel. (0265) 2310630 or 2331012/ iskcon.baroda@pamho.net

◆ **Bhubaneswar, Orissa** — N.H. No. 5, IRC Village, 751 015/ Tel. (0674) 2553517, 2553475, or 2554283

Chandigarh, Punjab — Hare Krishna Dham, Sector 36-B, 160 036/ Tel. (0172) 601590 or 603232/ iskcon.chandigarh@pamho.net

Chennai (Madras), TN — Hare Krishna Land, Bhaktivedanta Swami Road, Off ECR Road, Injambakkam, Chennai 600 041/ Tel. (044) 5019303 or 5019147/ iskconchennai@eth.net

◆ **Coimbatore, TN** — Jagannath Mandir, Hare Krishna Land, Aerodrome P.O., Opp. CIT, 641 014/ Tel. (0422) 2626509 or 2626508/ info@iskcon-coimbatore.org

Dwarka, Gujarat — Bharatiya Bhavan, Devi Bhavan Rd., 361 335/ Tel. (02892) 34606/ Fax: (02892) 34319

Guwahati, Assam — Ulubari Chariali, South Sarania, 781 007/ Tel. (0361) 2525963/ iskcon.guwahati@pamho.net

Haridwar, Uttaranchal — Prabhupada Ashram, G. House, Nai Basti, Mahadev Nagar, Bhimgoda/ Tel. (01334) 260818

Hyderabad, AP — Hare Krishna Land, Nampally Station Rd., 500 001/ Tel. (040) 24744969 or 24607089/ iskcon.hyderabad@pamho.net

Imphal, Manipur — Hare Krishna Land, Airport Rd., 795 001/ Tel. (0385) 2455245 or 2455247 or 2455693/ manimandir@sancharnet.in

Indore, MP — ISKCON, Nipania, Indore/ Tel. 9300474043/ mahaman.acbsp@pamho.net

Jaipur, Rajasthan — ISKCON Road, Opp. Vijay Path, Mansarovar, Jaipur 302 020 (mail: ISKCON, 84/230, Sant Namdev Marg, Opp. K.V. No. 5, Mansarovar, Jaipur 302 020)/ Tel. (0414) 2782765 or 2781860/ jaipur@pamho.net

Jammu, J&K — Srila Prabhupada Ashram, c/o Shankar Charitable Trust, Shakti Nagar, Near AG Office/ Tel. (01991) 233047

Kolkata (Calcutta), WB — 3C Albert Rd., 700 017 (behind Minto Park, opp. Birla High School)/ Tel. (033) 3028-9258 or -9280/ iskcon.calcutta@pamho.net

◆ **Kurukshetra, Haryana** — 369 Gudri Muhalla, Main Bazaar, 132 118/ Tel. (01744) 234806

Lucknow, UP — 1 Ashok Nagar, Guru Govind Singh Marg, 226 018/ Tel. (0522) 223556 or 271551

◆ **Mayapur, WB** — ISKCON, Shree Mayapur Chandrodaya Mandir, Shree Mayapur Dham, Dist. Nadia, 741 313/ Tel. (03472) 245239, 245240, or 245233/ Fax: (03472) 245238/ mayapur.chandrodaya@pamho.net

◆ **Mumbai (Bombay), Maharashtra** — Hare Krishna Land, Juhu 400 049/ Tel. (022) 26206860/ Fax: (022) 26205214/ info@iskconmumbai.com; guest.house.bombay@pamho.net

◆ **Mumbai, Maharashtra** — 7 K. M. Munshi Marg, Chowpatty 400 007 / Tel. (022) 23665500/ Fax: (022) 23665555/ info@radhagopinath.com

Mumbai, Maharashtra — Shristhi Complex, Mira Rd. (E), opposite Royal College, Dist. Thane, 401 107/ Tel. (022) 28454667 or 28454672/ jagjivan.gkg@pamho.net

Mysore, Karnataka — #31, 18th Cross, Jayanagar, 570 014/ Tel. (0821) 2500582 or 6567333/ mysore.iskcon@gmail.com

Nellore, AP — ISKCON City, Hare Krishna Rd., 524 004/ Tel. (0861) 2314577 or (092155) 36589/ sukadevaswami@gmail.com

◆ **New Delhi, UP** — Hare Krishna Hill, Sant Nagar Main Road, East of Kailash, 110 065/ Tel. (011) 2623-5133, 4, 5, 6, 7/ delhi@pamho.net; (Guesthouse) neel.sunder@pamho.net

◆ **New Delhi, UP** — 41/77, Punjabi Bagh (West), 110 026/ Tel. (011) 25222851 or 25227478 Noida, UP — A-5, Sector 33, opp. NTPC office, Noida 201 301/ Tel. (0120) 2506211/ vraja.bhakti.vilas.lok@pamho.net

Patna, Bihar — Arya Kumar Rd., Rajendra Nagar, 800 016/ Tel. (0612) 687637 or 685081/ kishna.kripa.jps@pamho.net

Pune, Maharashtra — 4 Tarapoor Rd., Camp, 411 001/ Tel. (020) 26332328 or 26361855/ iyfpune@vsnl.com

Puri, Orissa — Bhakti Kuti, Swargadwar, 752 001/ Tel. (06752) 231440

Raipur, Chhatisgarh — Hare Krishna Land, Alopi Nagar, Opposite Maharshi Vidyalaya, Tatibandh, Raipur 492 001/ Tel. (0771) 5037555/ iskconraipur@yahoo.com

Secunderabad, AP — 27 St. John's Rd., 500 026/ Tel. (040) 780-5232/ Fax: (040) 814021

Silchar, Assam — Ambikapatti, Silchar, Dist. Cachar, 788 004/ Tel. (03842) 34615

Sri Rangam, TN — 103 Amma Mandapam Rd., Sri Rangam, Trichy 620 006/ Tel. (0431) 2433945/ iskcon_srirangam@yahoo.com.in

Surat, Gujarat — Rander Rd., Jahangirpura, 395 005/ Tel. (0261) 765891, 765516, or 773386/ surat@pamho.net

◆ **Thiruvananthapuram (Trivandrum), Kerala** — Hospital Rd., Thycaud, 695 014/ Tel. (0471) 2328197/ jsdasa@yahoo.co.in
◆ **Tirupati, AP** — K.T. Rd., Vinayaka Nagar, 517 507/ Tel. (0877) 2230114 or 2230009/ revati.raman.jps@pamho.net (guesthouse: iskcon_ashram@yahoo.co.in)
Udhampur, J&K — Srila Prabhupada Ashram, Srila Prabhupada Marg, Srila Prabhupada Nagar 182 101/ Tel. (01992) 270298/ info@iskconudhampur.com
Ujjain, MP — Hare Krishna Land, Bharatpuri, 456 010/ Tel. (0734) 2535000 or 3205000/ Fax: (0734) 2536000/ iskcon.ujjain@pamhho.net
Varanasi, UP — ISKCON, B 27/80 Durgakund Rd., Near Durgakund Police Station, Varanasi 221 010/ Tel. (0542) 246422 or 222617
◆ **Vrindavan, UP** — Krishna-Balaram Mandir, Bhaktivedanta Swami Marg, Raman Reti, Mathura Dist., 281 124/ Tel. & Fax: (0565) 2540728/ iskcon.vrindavan@pamho.net; (Guesthouse:) Tel. (0565) 2540022; ramamani@sancharnet.in

ADDITIONAL RESTAURANT

Kolkata, WB — Govinda's, ISKCON House, 22 Gurusaday Rd., 700 019/ Tel. (033) 24756922, 24749009

EUROPE (partial list)*

Amsterdam — Van Hilligaertstraat 17, 1072 JX/ Tel. +31 (020) 675-1404 or -1694/ Fax: +31 (020) 675-1405/ amsterdam@pamho.net
Barcelona — Plaza Reial 12, Entlo 2, 08002/ Tel. +34 93 302-5194/ templobcn@hotmail.com
Bergamo, Italy — Villaggio Hare Krishna (da Medolago strada per Terno d'Isola), 24040 Chignolo d'Isola (BG)/
Tel. +39 (035) 4940706
Budapest — Lehel Street 15–17, 1039 Budapest/ Tel. +36 (01) 391-0435/ Fax: (01) 397-5219/ nai@pamho.net
Copenhagen — Skjulhoj Alle 44, 2720 Vanlose, Copenhagen/ Tel. +45 4828 6446/ Fax: +45 4828 7331/ iskcon.denmark@pamho.net
Grödinge, Sweden — Radha-Krishna Temple, Korsnäs Gård, 14792 Grödinge, Tel.+46 (08) 53029800/ Fax: +46 (08) 53025062 / bmd@pamho.net
Helsinki — Ruoholahdenkatu 24 D (III krs) 00180/ Tel. +358 (9) 694-9879 or -9837
◆ **Lisbon** — Rua Dona Estefânia, 91 R/C 1000 Lisboa/ Tel. & fax: +351(01) 314-0314 or 352-0038
Madrid — Espíritu Santo 19, 28004 Madrid/ Tel. +34 91 521-3096
Paris — 35 Rue Docteur Jean Vaquier, 93160 Noisy le Grand/ Tel. & fax: +33 (01) 4303-0951/ param.gati.swami@pamho.net
Prague — Jilova 290, Prague 5 - Zlicin 155 21/ Tel. +42 (02) 5795-0391/ info@harekrsna.cz
◆ **Radhadesh, Belgium** — Chateau de Petite Somme, 6940 Septon-Durbuy/ Tel. +32 (086) 322926 (restaurant: 321421)/ Fax: +32 (086) 322929/ radhadesh@pamho.net
◆ **Rome** — Govinda Centro Hare Krsna, via di Santa Maria del Pianto 16, 00186/ Tel. +39 (06) 68891540/ govinda.roma@harekrsna.it
◆ **Stockholm** — Fridhemsgatan 22, 11240/ Tel. +46 (08) 654-9002/ Fax: +46 (08) 650-881; Restaurant: Tel. & fax: +46 (08) 654-9004/ lokanatha@hotmail.com
Warsaw — Mysiadlo k. Warszawy, 05-500 Piaseczno, ul. Zakret 11/ Tel. +48 (022) 750-7797 or -8247/ Fax: +48 (022) 750-8249/ kryszna@post.pl
Zürich — Bergstrasse 54, 8030/ Tel. +41 (01) 262-3388/ Fax: +41 (01) 262-3114/ kgs@pamho.net

RURAL COMMUNITIES

France (La Nouvelle Mayapura) — Domaine d'Oublaisse, 36360, Lucay le Mâle/ Tel. +33 (02) 5440-2395/ Fax: +33 (02) 5440-2823/ oublaise@free.fr
Germany (Simhachalam) — Zielberg 20, 94118 Jandelsbrunn/ Tel. +49 (08583) 316/ info@simhachalam.de
Hungary (New Vraja-dhama) — Krisna-völgy, 8699 Somogyvamos, Fö u, 38/ Tel. & fax: +36 (085) 540-002 or 340-185/ info@krisnavolgy.hu
Italy (Villa Vrindavan) — Via Scopeti 108, 50026 San Casciano in Val di Pesa (FL)/ Tel. +39 (055) 820054/ Fax: +39 (055) 828470/ isvaripriya@libero.it
Spain (New Vraja Mandala) — (Santa Clara) Brihuega, Guadalajara/ Tel. +34 949 280436

ADDITIONAL RESTAURANTS

Barcelona — Restaurante Govinda, Plaza de la Villa de Madrid 4–5, 08002/ Tel. +34 (93) 318-7729
Copenhagen — Govinda's, Nørre Farimagsgade 82, DK-1364 Kbh K/ Tel. +45 3333 7444
Milan — Govinda's, Via Valpetrosa 5, 20123/ Tel. +39 (02) 862417
Oslo — Krishna's Cuisine, Kirkeveien 59B, 0364/ Tel. +47 (02) 260-6250
Zürich — Govinda Veda-Kultur, Preyergrasse 16, 8001/ Tel. & fax: +41 (01) 251-8859/ info@govinda-shop.ch

CIS (partial list)*

Kiev — 16, Zorany per., 04078/ Tel. +380 (044) 433-8312, or 434-7028 or -5533
Moscow — 8/3, Khoroshevskoye sh. (mail: P.O. Box 69), 125284/ Tel. +7 (095) 255-6711/ Tel. & fax: +7 (095) 945-3317

ASIA (partial list)*

Bangkok, Thailand — Soi3, Tanon Itsarapap, Toonburi/ Tel. +66 (02) 9445346 or (081) 4455401 or (089) 7810623/ swami.bvv.narasimha@pamho.net
Dhaka, Bangladesh — 5 Chandra Mohon Basak

St., Banagram,1203/ Tel. +880 (02) 236249/ Fax: (02) 837287/ iskcon_bangladesh@yahoo.com

Hong Kong — 6/F Oceanview Court, 27 Chatham Road South (mail: P.O. Box 98919)/ Tel. +852 (2) 739-6818/ Fax: +852 (2) 724-2186/ iskcon.hong.kong@pamho.net

Jakarta, Indonesia — Yayasan Radha-Govinda, P.O. Box 2694, Jakarta Pusat 10001/ Tel. +62 (021) 489-9646/ matsyads@bogor.wasantara.net.id

Katmandu, Nepal — Budhanilkantha (mail: GPO Box 3520)/ Tel. +977 (01) 373790 or 373786/ Fax: +977 (01) 372976 (Attn: ISKCON)/ iskcon@wlink.com.np

Kuala Lumpur, Malaysia — Lot 9901, Jalan Awan Jawa, Taman Yarl, 58200 Kuala Lumpur/ Tel. +60 (3) 7980-7355/ Fax: +60 (3) 7987-9901/ president@iskconkl.com

Manila, Philippines — Radha-Madhava Center, #9105 Banuyo St., San Antonio village, Makati City/ Tel. +63 (02) 8963357; Tel. & fax: +63 (02) 8901947/ iskconmanila@yahoo.com

Myitkyina, Myanmar — ISKCON Sri Jagannath Temple, Bogyoke Street, Shansu Taung, Myitkyina, Kachin State/ mahanadi@mptmail.net.mm

Tai Pei City, Taiwan — Ting Zhou Rd. Section 3, No. 192, 4F, Tai Pei City 100/ Tel. +886 (02) 2365-8641/ dayal.nitai.tkg@pamho.net

Tokyo, Japan — Subaru 1F, 4-19-6 Kamitakada, Nakano-ku, Tokyo 164-0002/ Tel. +81 (03) 5343- 9147 or (090) 6544-9284/ Fax: +81 (03) 5343-3812/ damodara@krishna.jp

LATIN AMERICA (partial list)*

Buenos Aires, Argentina — Centro Bhaktivedanta, Andonaegui 2054, Villa Urquiza, CP 1431/ Tel. +54 (01) 523-4232/ Fax: +54 (01) 523-8085/ iskcon-ba@gopalnet.com

Caracas, Venezuela — Av. Los Proceres (con Calle Marquez del Toro), San Bernardino/ Tel. +58 (212) 550-1818

Guayaquil, Ecuador — 6 de Marzo 226 and V. M. Rendon/ Tel. +593 (04) 308412 or 309420/ Fax: +564 302108/ gurumani@gu.pro.ec

◆ **Lima, Peru** — Schell 634 Miraflores/ Tel. +51 (014) 444-2871 **Mexico City, Mexico** — Tiburcio Montiel 45, Colonia San Miguel, Chapultepec D.F., 11850/ Tel. +52 (55) 5273-1953/ Fax: +52 (55) 52725944

Rio de Janeiro, Brazil — Rua Vilhena de Morais, 309, Barra da Tijuca, 22793-140/ Tel. +55 (021) 2491-1887/ sergio.carvalho@pobox.com

San Salvador, El Salvador — Calle Chiltiupan #39, Ciudad Merliot, Nueva San Salvador (mail: A.P. 1506)/ Tel. +503 2278-7613/ Fax: +503 2229-1472/ tulasikrishnadas@yahoo.com

São Paulo, Brazil — Rua do Paraiso, 694, 04103-000/Tel. +55 (011) 326-0975/ communicacaomandir@grupos.com.br

West Coast Demerara, Guyana — Sri Gaura Nitai Ashirvad Mandir, Lot "B," Nauville Flanders (Crane Old Road), West Coast Demerara/ Tel. +592 254 0494/ iskcon.guyana@yahoo.com

AFRICA (partial list)*

Accra, Ghana — Samsam Rd., Off Accra-Nsawam Hwy., Medie, Accra North (mail: P.O. Box 11686)/ Tel. & fax +233 (021) 229988/ srivas_bts@yahoo.co.in

Cape Town, South Africa — 17 St. Andrews Rd., Rondebosch 7700/ Tel. +27 (021) 6861179/ Fax: +27 (021) 686-8233/ cape.town@pamho.net

◆ **Durban, South Africa** — 50 Bhaktivedanta Swami Circle, Unit 5 (mail: P.O. Box 56003), Chatsworth, 4030/ Tel. +27 (031) 403-3328/ Fax: +27 (031) 403-4429/ iskcon.durban@pamho.net

Johannesburg, South Africa — 7971 Capricorn Ave. (entrance on Nirvana Drive East), Ext. 9, Lenasia (mail: P.O. Box 926, Lenasia 1820)/ Tel. +27 (011) 854-1975 or 7969/ iskconjh@iafrica.com

Lagos, Nigeria — 12, Gani Williams Close, off Osolo Way, Ajao Estate, International Airport Rd. (mail: P.O. Box 8793, Marina)/ Tel. +234 (01) 7744926 or 7928906/ bdds.bts@pamho.net

Mombasa, Kenya — Hare Krishna House, Sauti Ya Kenya and Kisumu Rds. (mail: P.O. Box 82224, Mombasa)/ Tel. +254 (011) 312248

Nairobi, Kenya — Muhuroni Close, off West Nagara Rd. (mail: P.O. Box 28946)/ Tel. +254 (203) 744365/ Fax: +254 (203) 740957/ iskcon_nairobi@yahoo.com

◆ **Phoenix, Mauritius** — Hare Krishna Land, Pont Fer (mail: P.O. Box 108, Quartre Bornes)/ Tel. +230 696-5804/ Fax: +230 696-8576/ iskcon.hkl@intnet.mu

Port Harcourt, Nigeria — Umuebule 11, 2nd tarred road, Etche (mail: P.O. Box 4429, Trans Amadi)/ Tel. +234 08033215096/ canakyaus@yahoo.com

Pretoria, South Africa — 1189 Church St., Hatfield, 0083 (mail: P.O. Box 14077, Hatfield, 0028)/ Tel. & fax: +27 (12) 342-6216/ iskconpt@global.co.za

RURAL COMMUNITY

Mauritius (ISKCON Vedic Farm) — Hare Krishna Rd., Vrindaban/ Tel. +230 418-3185 or 418-3955/ Fax: +230 418-6470

***The full list is always available at Krishna.com, where it also includes Krishna conscious gatherings.**

Far from a Center? Call us at 1-800-927-4152. Or contact us on the Internet
http://www.krishna.com • E-mail: bbt.usa@krishna.com

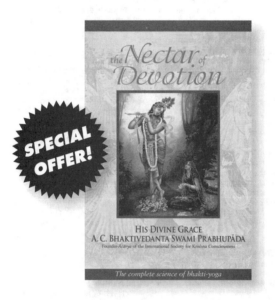

The Bhaktivedanta
Book Trust
CATALOG